savour

AMBER LOCKE

savour

SENSATIONAL SOUPS TO FULFIL & FORTIFY

MITCHELL BEAZLEY

CONTENTS

ABOUT ME

My love of fruit and vegetables stems from my childhood and growing up with enthusiastic gardeners as parents. We always had a huge vegetable garden at every house we lived in and a seemingly constant, year-round supply of seasonal fruit and vegetables. I remember the thrill of digging up new potatoes as a child, it felt like discovering treasure as I carefully unearthed the small golden-yellow tubers and piled them into a bucket with glee. I loved picking herbs, tomatoes, lettuce, raspberries and peas in the summer and gathering apples and plums from the orchard and dessert grapes from the vine in the autumn.

My parents would spend hours and hours tending to the different veg, often growing them from seed, and the garden was always immaculately kept and beautiful to look at. Alongside their favourite fruit and veg would be new and experimental varieties such as rainbow chard, ornamental pumpkins or, one year, Siberian, American and cold-climate varieties of tomato.

My mother is also a great cook so not only did I grow up surrounded by a bounty of fresh produce, I was taught how to cook with it, too. One of her theories is that every meal should feature at least seven different colours for it to be properly healthy, so the food that she prepares is not only garden-fresh but super colourful, too. I guess some of her enthusiasm rubbed off on me.

My diet now is predominantly vegetable-based and I'm also a big raw food advocate and enthusiast. However, I do appreciate the merits of cooked vegetables too, especially the grounding and comforting role they can play in the colder autumn and winter months. So soups and salads are the two types of dishes I most commonly eat.

The soup I remember most fondly from my childhood is celery soup, which my mother would make for me as a treat (see my Celery Soup version on page 76). I loved its natural creaminess when blended and its slightly salty, lemony flavour. When I was a little older,

she'd serve it with crushed pink peppercorns, which I thought was the height of sophistication aged ten.

In more recent years, certain soups stick in my memory: a wild mushroom soup with the most amazing depth of flavour served at a local Derbyshire restaurant (see my Mixed Mushroom soup version on page 68); a beautiful fish bouillabaisse at La Residencia hotel in Mallorca; a fabulous onion soup at a French restaurant on a recent trip to New York; and even the super-quick tomato and rice soup that I frequently make when I'm pressed for time (see the totally raw, totally vegan version Tomato Cauli Rice Soup on page 51)...all these soups and many more hold memories of my life.

ABOUT THIS BOOK

This book showcases my love of fruit and vegetables and one of my favourite ways to serve them...in colourful and nutritious soups.

The soups you will find here are all vegan – some raw, some cooked and some sweet – but all come with alternative serving ideas, many of which will appeal to omnivores. You'll find a soup for every colour of the rainbow, which illustrates the amazing and diverse spectrum of colours that occur naturally in nature and shows how easy it really can be to 'eat – or drink – the rainbow.'

I've also included staple recipes for base stocks, health information on ingredients, storage and serving tips, kitchen kit advice, and a collection of toppings, drizzles and sprinkles to perk up the look, taste, texture and nutritional value of your soups.

So, in praise of fruit and vegetables, this book is a true celebration of their versatility, the vital role they play in our diets, and how they help us to stay healthy. I hope you'll find plenty to entertain and inspire...and that you, like me, also enjoy the beauty of soup.

Amber

WHY SOUP?

A humble bowl of soup is one of the most versatile of dishes; there's nothing quite like spooning up warm goodness on a cold winter's day, sipping a light chilled soup to refresh in the summer months, or hugging a mug of comforting broth if you're feeling under the weather. A simple bowl of soup has the ability to do far more than nourish our bodies; it has the restorative and comforting power to revive us and soothe the soul, too.

Whether served warm or chilled, as a snack or main meal, soups are readily adaptable. Most can be made more substantial with extra veg, added protein and carbs, or spruced up with a selection of interesting toppings – they're almost the little black dress equivalent of the culinary world.

Usually a healthy choice, soups are more often than not vegetable-based and provide a great opportunity to sneak in extra veg. I find a handful of finely grated raw carrot or courgette stirred into a flavoursome soup just before serving can often go undetected. They're economic to make, too, and can be a wonderful way of using up odds and ends in the fridge, leftover cooked veg, or utilizing slightly wilted specimens that you might otherwise discard.

If you're watching your weight, soups can be your best friend in the kitchen – they quickly assuage hunger and leave you feeling satisfied for longer. A raw soup can be whipped up in minutes so is ideal if you're feeling ravenous, or if made in bulk and frozen in portions, a soup can take mere minutes to defrost and serve up. Similarly, if you crave something sweet, my recipes for low-sugar fresh fruit soups (see pages 112–125) are the perfect antidote.

TYPES OF SOUP

Gazpacho, chowder, mulligatawny, vichyssoise, borscht, velouté, pho, minestrone, broth, ramen, potage, bisque, consommé...these names can define the ingredients in a soup, its texture, style of cooking, and/or the country of origin. But what is clear is that soup comes in many guises to suit every eating occasion or mood. There are delicate, clear broths; rustic, chunky, soups-cum-stews; or silky-smooth versions with a velvety texture and creamy mouthfeel. Soups can be healthy, cleansing and nourishing or luxurious and indulgent, as well as quick to prepare or cooked slowly over a long period of time. Whatever the type, all good soups start with some basic, fresh ingredients and a little know-how...

WHAT MAKES A GOOD SOUP?

As with any recipe, a good soup normally begins with good ingredients. For me, the following are key:

☀ FRUIT & VEGETABLES: I like to use organic fruit and vegetables whenever possible. These often have the best flavour and you don't need to peel them. Just scrub the veg, including beetroots, carrots, parsnips, sweet potatoes and potatoes, clean before use. Keeping the skins on means you retain a lot of the nutrients. If using non-organic veg, it's best to peel them first.

☀ COOKING OIL: I generally try to use as little additional oil as possible and when sautéing vegetables for a soup I'll often steam-fry them (see Making, Serving & Storing Tips opposite). My preferred oil is coconut as it has many health benefits and a high smoke point. The coconut flavour is normally undetectable, but for more delicately flavoured soups I opt for a light olive oil.

☀ STOCK: I tend to use four basic types of stock (see pages 14–17). The Cooked Vegetable Stock is the one I go to for most soups and it's even delicious drunk on its own like a broth. For more delicately flavoured soups I'll use the light vegetable stock, or when I want to add other flavourings or aromatics. If I'm making a Thai-style soup, for instance, I may add lemon grass, coriander or fresh ginger to the light stock, or include star anise to make a Chinese-inspired broth. The Dehydrated Vegetable Stock Powder is a great 'instant' stock when in a hurry or to give a flavour boost to a soup, while the Raw Vegetable Stock is a must for raw soups and to give a fresh-tasting flavour boost to other types of soup, stews and sauces.

☀ FINISHING TOUCHES: a few well-chosen extras can make all the difference to a soup, boosting its nutritional value and transforming it into something special. Toppings don't have to be elaborate: a handful of sprouted seeds, crushed dry-roasted peanuts or crunchy sourdough croûtons scattered over the top are often enough. A spoonful of grated carrot, a few chopped herbs, a drizzle of yogurt or cream, or a sprinkle of spices can all lift and enliven a bowl of soup. (See pages 128–139 for more ideas.)

HOW TO BLEND A SOUP

Of course some soups don't require blending – consommé, miso or more chunky stew-like soups – but I prefer to blend my soups and the method I use depends on the texture I want to achieve.

☀ My food processor gives a coarse-textured soup as the ingredients are chopped rather than blended, which perfectly suits tomato soups and some vegetable soups that I don't want to be silky smooth.

❄ My high-speed, hand-held stick and immersion blenders produce velvety-smooth soups. I'll use one over the other depending on the amount I'm making – the latter being most suitable for smaller quantities. I also use my high-speed blender for raw soups: just pop the raw ingredients and liquid into the jug and press blend. Mine also has a 'soup' function, where the heat of the spinning blades gently heats the liquid so you are left with a warm but technically 'raw' soup.

❄ You can also use a mouli to purée your soups – it gives a smooth, fine-textured end result.

MAKING, SERVING & STORING TIPS

Now you've got your base ingredients and blending method sorted, here are a few tips to help you get the most out of your soup:

❄ Always make more than you need. Soups are great to stash away in the freezer for a quick, healthy meal.

❄ Save up vegetable trimmings, scraps or stems and use to make a full-flavoured vegetable stock.

❄ Use a good stock (see pages 14–17). The lifeblood of a soup, a well-flavoured, preferably homemade, vegetable stock will give a great depth of flavour and reduce the need for additional salt or flavourings.

❄ Steam-fry your vegetables to reduce the amount of oil needed: sauté them in a small amount of oil, cover with a lid and let them steam-cook for a few minutes until tender. The natural moisture in the vegetables is normally enough to create a steamy atmosphere in the pan, otherwise add a splash of water or stock.

❄ Bulk out a soup: add grated raw vegetables or chopped up cooked veg just before serving. Also try adding cooked wholegrains including brown rice, lentils, barley, quinoa, beans and chickpeas. These add fibre and give a boost of plant-based protein.

❄ Want a dairy-free creamy taste and texture? Add a handful of soaked cashew nuts before blending. Cooked cauliflower, potato, white beans, non-dairy yogurt or a nut-based milk or cream will also work.

❄ Need to thicken a soup? Blend in cooked vegetables such as potatoes, or stir in a handful of rice or oats and simmer until cooked. Adding chunks of stale bread or breadcrumbs will absorb some of the liquid. Cornflour is also an option: mix 1 teaspoon cornflour with 1 tablespoon cold water to a smooth paste. Stir into the soup and simmer, stirring constantly, until thickened.

❄ Soup too salty? Starchy food such as potatoes, rice, pasta or noodles are a great rescue remedy – they absorb some of the salt and their bland flavour helps balance the flavour. A pinch of sugar or the acidity from a little lemon juice or vinegar can help, too.

❄ Never let your soup boil. Over-heating or over-cooking can turn vegetables mushy, dull the flavour and cause nutrient loss. The exceptions are soups that include pulses or carbs such as pasta.

❄ To lift the flavour of a soup, particularly a tomato-based one, add a squeeze of lemon juice or a little finely grated zest at the end of the cooking time.

❄ To enrich a soup, try a dollop of cream cheese, milk or cream. Add a Parmesan rind to a tomato-based soup, or stir in a tablespoon of sherry, brandy, or a knob of butter or nut butter for an instant rich taste.

❄ Spices are an easy way to add interest to a soup. I'll often add them when I sauté the vegetables to release their flavour and fragrance. Be careful not to burn them, as they can turn bitter.

❄ Slow-cookers are perfect for soups that require a long cooking time, such as ones using dried pulses.

❄ Soup can improve with keeping. Making it a day ahead can help the flavours to meld and develop.

❄ Making a large batch of soup with the intention of saving some? Ensure it cools down completely before you store it. Fresh vegetable-based soups normally keep well in an airtight container in the fridge for two to three days and in the freezer for up to one month, after which time the flavours start to degrade. Store soups in freezer-proof containers or individually portioned zip-lock bags for easy defrosting.

❄ When it comes to presentation, there are no hard-and-fast rules but I like to serve my soups in particular vessels – it all adds to the look. Thin soups suit daintier bowls or teacups; heartier, chunky soups work in flat, wide bowls or mugs; chilled or sweet soups can be lovely served in glasses, while shot glasses work for palate-cleansing or canapé-style soups.

TOOL KIT

You don't need much in the way of kitchen tools to make soup – just a chopping board, sharp knife, saucepan and possibly a blender. For a more extensive tool kit that includes equipment to make toppings and extras, I would include:

* High-speed blender
* Hand-held stick or immersion blender
* Food processor with an 'S' blade and different discs for grating
* Microplane graters with different blades for zesting and coarse grating
* Mandoline with various blades
* Selection of sharp knives
* Serrated or zig-zag bladed wave knife
* 'V' blade channel knifes)
* Pastry cutters (various shapes)
* Various measuring jugs and spoons
* Citrus zester
* Melon ballers; mini and standard-sized
* Citrus juicer and reamer
* Julienne peeler
* Vegetable peeler
* Leaf stripper
* A spice grinder/coffee bean mill
* Spiralizer
* Stockpot with lid
* Saucepan with lid
* Sauté pan with lid
* Baking tray
* Wooden spoons, fish slice, tongs
* Chopping boards

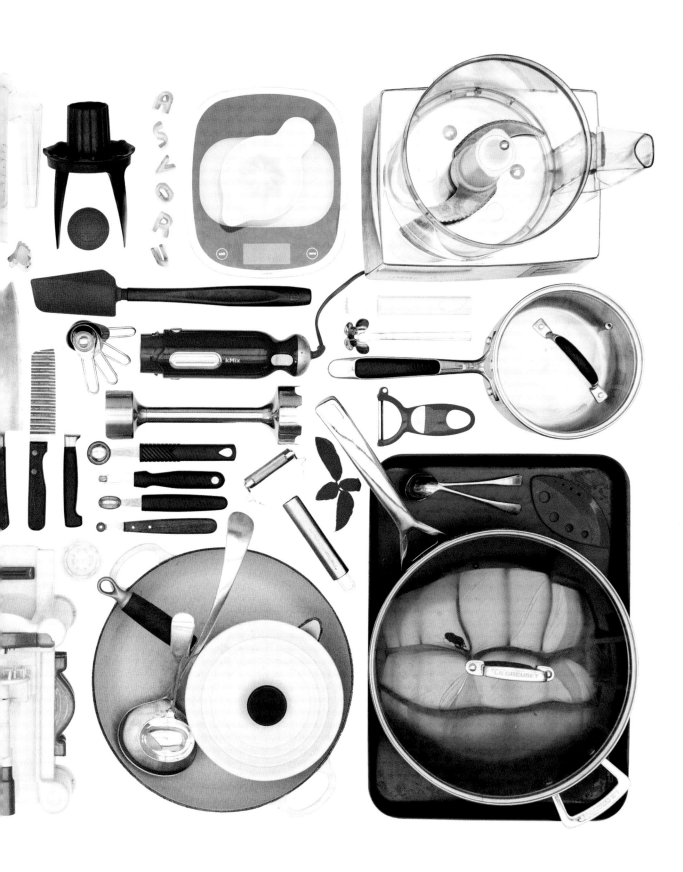

FINISHING TOUCHES

I've already touched on this earlier (see page 8), but a topping can transform an ordinary soup into something a bit special as well as add additional nutrients, visual interest, texture and flavour. The following gives you some great ideas to dollop, drizzle, spoon, sprinkle or scatter on top of your soups (also see Toppings & Sprinkles pages 128–139):

✳ OILS: good extra virgin olive oil, avocado oil, herb oil and flavoured oil, including lemon, chilli and sesame oil.

✳ VINEGARS: balsamic and white balsamic vinegar.

✳ SAUCES: homemade Sriracha (see page 135), soy sauce, teriyaki sauce, Worcestershire sauce, aioli, harissa, red and green Thai curry paste, pesto, salsa, mustard, tahini.

✳ YOGURT & CREAM: Greek yogurt, goats' milk yogurt, Raw Almond Yogurt (see page 137), Raw Cashew Cream (see page 138), soured cream, raita, labneh.

✳ PROTEIN: marinated tofu or tempeh, shredded meat, such as cooked chicken, pork or beef, crumbled crispy bacon, frazzled chorizo, mini meatballs.

✳ CHEESE: grated hard cheese, diced paneer, marinated feta, diced fresh mozzarella or burrata, Parmesan crisps.

✳ EGGS: poached or fried eggs, hard-boiled quail's eggs, ribbons of pancake or omelette, bite-sized pieces of frittata.

✳ FISH: flaked salmon or smoked mackerel, slivers of smoked salmon, cooked brown shrimps, mini fish cakes, flaked crabmeat.

✳ RAW VEG: finely shredded greens, such as spinach leaves, Swiss chard or cabbage, grated or spiralized courgette, carrot, beetroot or sweet potato, Raw Veg Confetti (see page 31), shaved truffles, peas, sweetcorn, finely sliced fennel or asparagus, shaved parsnip, shredded leeks, 'riced' courgette or cauliflower.

✳ RAW FRUIT: pomegranate seeds, finely diced avocado or tomato, finely sliced fresh chilli, citrus zest, apple matchsticks, frozen mixed berries.

✳ DRIED VEG: dehydrated vegetable crisps or powders (see page 131), seaweed confetti or spaghetti.

✳ PRESERVED & CURED: olives, capers, juniper berries, kimchi, sauerkraut, sun-dried tomatoes, peppadew peppers.

✳ COOKED TOPPINGS: gnocchi, dumplings, gyoza, wontons, gougères, Matzo Balls (see page 101), falafel.

✳ NUTS & SEEDS: whole, crushed or toasted nuts and seeds; sweet or Savoury Granola (see page 131); poppy seeds, hemp seeds, sunflower seeds, sesame seeds, pine nuts, flaked almonds, crushed dry-roasted peanuts.

✳ CROUTONS: sourdough, rye bread, potato, sweet potato, polenta, cheese-topped toasts.

✳ SUPERFOODS: spirulina powder, bee pollen, flaxseeds, goji berries.

✳ CRISPS: homemade root veg crisps, tortilla chips.

✳ COOKED GRAINS/SEEDS/PULSES: faro, freekeh, buckwheat, quinoa, amaranth, couscous, brown rice, lentils, beans, barley, chickpeas.

✳ COOKED VEG: roast vegetables, sweet potato wedges, Cauliflower Steaks (see page 134), caramelized or crispy onions; steamed veg, such as sugar snap peas, green beans and broccoli florets; kale chips, crispy veg tempura, mini rosti and Crispy Sprout Leaves (see page 132).

✳ SPROUTING SEEDS: pea shoots, sunflower sprouts, mixed sprouting seeds.

✳ SPICES: sumac, saffron, paprika and dried chilli flakes; spice mixes, such as Za'atar, Panch Phoran and Dukkah (see page 128), garam masala and ras-el-hanout; whole spices, including mustard seeds, pink peppercorns, caraway, fennel, cumin, nigella and juniper.

✳ HERBS: fresh herbs, including mint, basil, parsley, dill, thyme and chives, dried herbs and dried herb powders.

✳ EDIBLE FLOWERS: fresh flowers, such as roses, primroses, fuchsias, marigolds, violets, borage, and wild garlic flowers, dried flowers, including rose petals, calendula and hibiscus.

✳ DRIED FRUIT: cranberries, barberries, freeze-dried raspberries and strawberries, sun-dried tomatoes.

WHAT MAKES A GOOD STOCK?

A good stock really can be liquid gold in the kitchen. Just one ladleful has the ability to transform – and infuse flavour and fragrance into – many dishes, including stews, sauces and risottos.

A great-tasting stock doesn't have to be made out of bones to have depth of flavour and richness. A vegetable-based stock can be equally tasty, even if the layers of flavours are a little less complex.

Veggie stock can be exceptionally nutritious and drinkable. Just add a few rice noodles, some wilted greens or finely-grated raw veg and you have a comforting, restorative and rejuvenating meal in minutes.

I typically make vegetable stocks in four different ways: a cooked stock, a quick light stock, a raw stock and a dehydrated vegetable powder stock. Recipes for all are included on the following pages.

TIPS FOR MAKING COOKED VEGETABLE STOCK:

✳ It sounds obvious but always start with the freshest (preferably organic) ingredients: big-flavoured fruit and vegetables, plus a selection of herbs and spices.

✳ To retain as many nutrients and flavours as possible, don't boil your stock. Start with cold water and slowly bring to a simmer.

✳ Cut the vegetables into small pieces, rather than large chunks. This shortens the cooking time and helps to extract the flavours and preserve vitamins and minerals.

✳ For a richer flavour and deeper colour, lightly sauté the onion, carrot and celery in a little oil until browned before you add them to the stock pot.

✳ Keep any leftover herb stems to use in stocks as these are loaded with flavour.

✳ If you want a clear stock, don't use starchy vegetables like potatoes that can thicken the stock and make it go cloudy.

✳ Unless you're making the stock for a specific recipe, leave out stronger flavours, such as garlic, fennel, seaweed, whole spices, lemon grass, ginger and chillies. These can unbalance the flavour and be overpowering if used in a more delicate-tasting soup

✳ Some ingredients can act as subtle flavour enhancers without being too strong. Mushrooms give a lovely, rich umami taste, whereas a bouquet garni (a bundle of different herbs tied together) made with parsley, thyme, bay leaves, rosemary and/or marjoram will provide a wonderful herbal infusion and fragrance.

✳ To keep the stock clear and fresh-tasting, occasionally skim off any 'scum' or froth that rises to the surface using a spoon or fine mesh strainer.

✳ Strain your stock when ready using a chinois, a muslin-lined sieve or a nut milk bag.

✳ Store the stock in an airtight container in the fridge or freezer. If freezing, leave the stock to cool completely before pouring into smaller containers or an ice-cube tray – this makes for quick and easy defrosting.

COOKED VEGETABLE STOCK

This is my highly customizable basic stock recipe. If I'm making it for a specific soup, I tend to keep to the three magic ingredients of carrot, onion and celery and then choose the other ingredients to suit the flavour of the soup I'm making.

4 small carrots, cut into medium dice

3 celery sticks, cut into medium dice

2 large onions or 2 medium leeks, cut in half

1 bay leaf

1 small bunch of mixed herbs, such as parsley, thyme and rosemary

2 tsp black peppercorns

2 litres (3½ pints) water

Place the carrots, celery and onions in a large saucepan with the bay leaf, herbs and peppercorns and pour over the measured water. The water should cover the vegetables completely by 5–8cm (2–3¼in); you might need to add more depending on the size of your pan.

Bring to a gentle simmer and cook for 40–50 minutes, occasionally skimming away any froth that rises to the surface, until the stock tastes rich and full; take care not to overcook the vegetables or the flavour will become stale and flat.

Strain the stock, discarding the solids, and use straightaway or store in an airtight container in the fridge for up to 1 week, or freeze for 1–2 months.

QUICK 'NO-RECIPE' LIGHT VEGETABLE STOCK

This handy broth can be used as a base for soups, sauces or stews, or just drunk on its own as a restorative elixir. It's a simple, no-recipe formula that's easy to prepare and can be frozen in ice-cube trays for quick defrosting.

It's an excellent way to use up any odds and ends, veg scraps or wilting veg in the fridge, and since the broth is only cooked briefly it's fine to add strongly flavoured veg, such as cabbage or broccoli, which you would normally avoid in a stock. For a filling quick meal, add other types of veg, cooked protein and carbs.

3 large handfuls of mixed vegetables, such as carrots, celery, onions, leeks, cauliflower, cabbage and broccoli, cut into small pieces

1 small handful of herbs, such as thyme, parsley and rosemary

1 small handful of other flavourings, such as 6–7 black peppercorns, 1–2 bay leaves, 1 large garlic clove, 1 small dried chilli, 1 small piece fresh root ginger or a few dried mushrooms

salt and pepper

Place the vegetables in a large saucepan with the herbs and your choice of flavourings, such as bay leaves and peppercorns.

Cover with water and bring to the boil, then turn the heat down and simmer for 15–20 minutes until the vegetables are tender but not overcooked.

Strain the liquid (discarding the herbs, flavourings and vegetables), season to taste with salt and pepper and either use straightaway or leave to cool.

Cover and store in an airtight container in the fridge for 3–5 days, or store in the freezer for 1–3 months.

RAW VEGETABLE STOCK

My raw veg stock adds a flavour boost to raw soups and salad dressings and, if I'm feeling run down, I like to drink a straight shot of it as an elixir. I make it by juicing a variety of fruits, vegetables, herbs and spices to create a rich, intense juice with a mixture of super-concentrated flavours.

As with the Cooked Vegetable Stock (see page 15), this raw alternative can be treated as a foundation recipe to which you add other ingredients depending on how you're going to use it. For instance, if I'm using it as a stock for a spicy Asian-style soup, I might add a thumb-sized piece of fresh turmeric, a handful of fresh coriander, ¼ teaspoon cumin seeds and a stalk of lemon grass. Fennel also gives it an aniseedy kick, yet unlike the cooked veg stock, I rarely add carrot as it can be very sweet and I prefer to keep the flavours clean and savoury.

⅓ red onion, peeled, or ½ large leek, trimmed

2–3 garlic cloves, peeled and left whole

2–3cm (¾–1¼in) piece fresh root ginger, peeled

4 celery sticks

1 jalapeño chilli or red or green chilli, deseeded if you prefer less heat

1 small bunch of mixed herbs, such as parsley, basil, coriander, dill, rosemary and marjoram

sea salt flakes

Run all the ingredients through a slow juicer. Pour the liquid into a large jug or bowl, stir and season to taste with salt, if desired. Alternatively, add extra juiced celery as it is naturally high in salt. Store in an airtight container in the fridge for 1–2 days.

DEHYDRATED VEGETABLE STOCK POWDER

It's always handy to have a pot of instant vegetable stock powder as part of your store cupboard essentials – shop-bought varieties can taste a bit musty or overly salty and by making your own you know exactly what's in it. The vegetables all need to be washed, dried and very thinly sliced before they are dehydrated; a mandoline is perfect for slicing.

4 large carrots, very thinly sliced

2 large red onions, very thinly sliced

2 large courgettes, very thinly sliced

2 red peppers, deseeded and very thinly sliced

3–4 large mushrooms, very thinly sliced

3–4 celery sticks, very thinly sliced

4 large tomatoes, very thinly sliced

4 garlic cloves, very thinly sliced

1 small handful of mixed herb leaves, such as parsley, dill, coriander and oregano

1 tsp ground paprika

1 tsp kelp powder

2 tsp sea salt flakes, or to taste

pepper

Preheat the oven to 65°C (150°F) Gas Mark ¼ or as low as your oven will go. Alternatively, use a dehydrator and follow the instructions for your model.

Arrange the prepared vegetables and herbs in a single layer on wire racks set inside or on top of baking trays.

Place in the oven for 3–5 hours, turning once, or until completely dry and brittle; you may need to do this in batches. Remove from the oven and leave to cool completely.

Using a high-speed blender, coffee mill or spice grinder, blitz the dehydrated ingredients in batches to a fine powder. Tip the powder into a large bowl, then stir in the paprika, kelp powder, salt and pepper and mix well to combine. Season to taste with extra salt and pepper, if needed.

To use, stir the stock powder directly into warm liquids, sauces and stews or add 2 teaspoons stock powder to a heatproof jug and pour in 300ml (10fl oz) boiling water, then stir to combine. Taste and add more stock powder, if needed.

Store the powder in an airtight container in a cool place for up to 2 months.

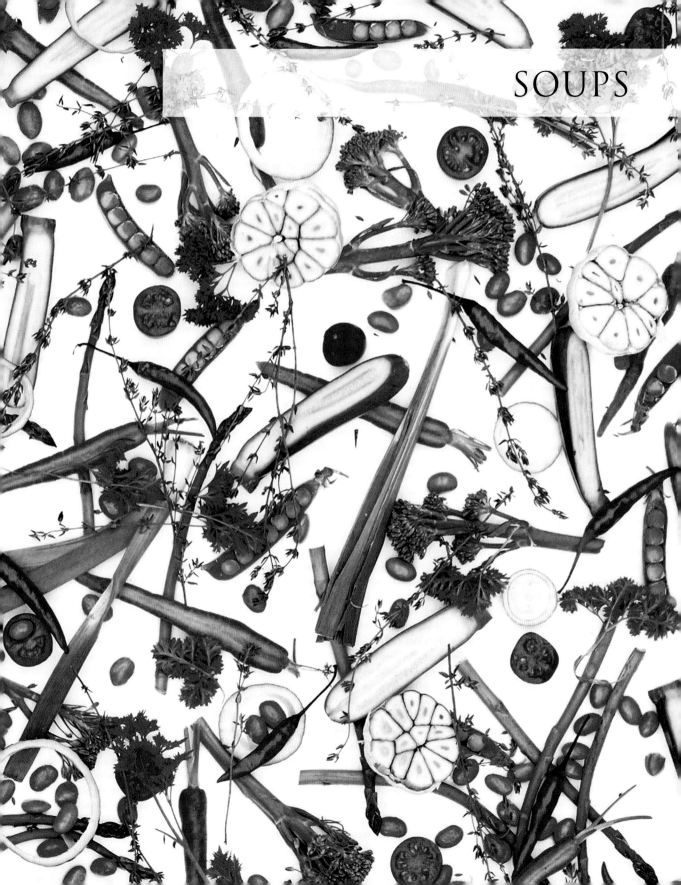

CURRIED GREENS & COCONUT SOUP

This mixed greens soup is mildly hot and delicately perfumed with spices.
I first ate a version of this at a beachside cookery class while on holiday in the
Maldives. The base of the soup can be made in advance and the cooked green
veg added at the last minute.

SERVES 2-3

2 tbsp olive oil ✳ 1 large onion, finely chopped

5cm (2in) piece fresh root ginger, peeled and finely chopped

3 garlic cloves, finely chopped ✳ 20g (¾oz) curry leaves

2 cinnamon sticks, broken in half if large ✳ 5 cardamom pods, bruised

5 whole cloves ✳ ½ tsp garam masala ✳ ½ tsp ground turmeric

¼ tsp ground cumin ✳ 1 tbsp tomato paste

200ml (7fl oz) coconut cream ✳ 200ml (7fl oz) hot Cooked Vegetable Stock (see page 15)

750g (1lb 10 oz) mixed greens (broccoli florets, green beans, bok choy, courgettes, asparagus,
Swiss chard, spinach, fennel…whatever you have to hand), roughly chopped or thinly sliced

salt and pepper

TO SERVE

3–4 tbsp chopped coriander leaves

2–3 tbsp freshly grated or shaved coconut ✳ 2 limes, cut into wedges

Heat the oil in a large sauté pan, add the onion and fry gently until translucent.

Add the ginger, garlic, curry leaves and spices and cook, stirring constantly, for a few
minutes until they release their fragrance. Stir in the tomato paste, coconut cream and stock
then simmer for 5 minutes or until thickened. Season to taste with salt and pepper.

Gently steam (or sauté) the greens, or keep them raw if preferred.
Divide the greens between serving bowls, saving some to garnish.

To serve, ladle the soup over the greens. Top each serving with the reserved greens,
the coriander and coconut, with wedges of lime for squeezing over.

Nutrition tip

Top up your levels of folic acid, vitamin C and antioxidants with this green-laden soup.
The coconut milk supplies MCTs (medium chain triglycerides),
which can help improve fat-to-muscle ratios in the body.

TRY ADDING prawns, fresh tuna or shredded chicken for a protein boost.

VELVETY BEETROOT SOUP

This smooth, vibrant soup is great for your health thanks to the beetroot – an amazing nutritional powerhouse. The crisp Paneer Bites (see page 134) and Popped Pumpkin Seeds (see page 130) give a crunchy contrast to the velvety-textured soup.

SERVES 2-3

6 large raw beetroots, scrubbed, stems and leaves removed

400ml (14fl oz) hot Cooked Vegetable Stock (see page 15) ❋ juice of ½ lemon

3–4 tbsp Raw Almond Yogurt (see page 137) or yogurt of your choice

salt and pepper

TO SERVE

½ tsp grated fresh horseradish

3 tbsp Raw Soured Cashew Cream (see page 138)

Marinated 'Paneer Bites' (see page 134) ❋ Popped Pumpkin Seeds (see page 130)

dill sprigs, to garnish

Place the beetroots in a large saucepan, cover with cold water and bring to the boil. Cook the beetroots, covered, at a robust simmer for 50–60 minutes until tender, then drain and leave to cool.

When cool enough to handle, remove the skins – they should slip off quite easily but use rubber gloves to prevent the juice staining your fingers. Chop the beetroot into large chunks.

Place the beetroot in the bowl of a food processor with the other ingredients and blitz to a silky smooth consistency. You could use a stick blender, but beware the potentially permanent purple splatters! Season to taste with salt and pepper, and refrigerate for 2–3 hours if serving chilled.

Before serving, mix the horseradish with the soured cream.

To serve, ladle the soup into bowls and top with the paneer bites, pumpkin seeds and a drizzle of the horseradish cream. Garnish with a sprig of dill before enjoying warm or chilled.

Nutrition tip

This soup really maxes out on beetroot benefits. Perhaps tuck into a bowl or two before a run if you want to have a go at improving your time!

❋

SAVE THE BEETROOT STEMS AND LEAVES – they are a great source of nutrition. Juice and drink the stems and use the raw leaves in a salad or finely chopped to garnish the soup – beetroot leaves have more iron than spinach!

MISO BROTHS

Miso soup is so easy to make and I love serving it with a buffet of fixin's to allow everyone to add their own choice of toppings, flavourings and sprinkles. The added extras can provide a contrast of taste, texture and colour, so it's good to offer a few different options, including crunchy vegetables, soft noodles or spicy fresh ginger.

SERVES 3-4

800ml (1⅓ pints) Vegan Dashi (see page 138)

1 tbsp dried seaweed, such as nori or wakame

2 tbsp miso paste (white or dark, or a mixture of both)

2–3 spring onions, finely sliced ✳ 1–2 tsp sesame oil

salt and pepper

TO SERVE

a selection of fixin's, including finely sliced radishes, spiralized carrots or courgettes, cucumber noodles or ribbons, celery leaves, finely sliced leeks, mushrooms or chillies, edamame beans, finely grated fresh root ginger, cooked glass or soba noodles and sliced bok choy

Pour the dashi into a large saucepan and bring almost to the boil.
Add the seaweed and simmer for 2 minutes.

Put the miso paste in a small bowl, add 2 tablespoons of the dashi broth and whisk until dissolved and then pour it back into the pan. Add the spring onions and simmer briefly. Season to taste with salt and pepper.

To serve, pour into individual glass cups or bowls, top with the fixin's of your choice, and add a drizzle of sesame oil.

Nutrition tip

Miso paste is a fermented food that can help the good bacteria in your gut to thrive.
These good bacteria help keep your digestive and immune systems healthy.

ADD cubes of tofu for added protein.
STIR IN cooked wild or brown rice for a more substantial meal.
SERVE AS a Japanese vegetable stew – simmer the fixin's in the soup instead of separately.

CREAMY CHICKPEA SOUP

The mild flavour of the chickpeas is spiced with sumac, while the capers give
a nice briny tang. Chickpeas are high in protein and become rich, creamy
and comforting when they're blended.

SERVES 3-4

200g (7oz) dried chickpeas ✳ 1 tbsp olive oil or coconut oil

1 onion, finely chopped ✳ 1 carrot, finely chopped

2 celery sticks, finely chopped ✳ 1–2 garlic cloves, finely chopped

1 tsp sumac, plus extra for sprinkling

350ml (12fl oz) hot Cooked Vegetable Stock (see page 15)

1–2 tbsp preserved capers, rinsed and drained, plus extra to garnish

salt and pepper

Put the chickpeas in a bowl, cover with plenty of cold water and leave to soak overnight,
then drain.

Place the chickpeas in a large saucepan and cover with fresh cold water. Bring to the boil,
then turn the heat down and simmer for about 1 hour, or until tender. Drain the chickpeas
and set aside until ready to use.

Heat the oil in a large saucepan, add the onion, carrot, celery, garlic and sumac and fry gently
until the vegetables have softened. Add the cooked chickpeas, reserving a few to garnish,
and stock and simmer for a few minutes to heat through. Stir in the capers.

Remove the pan from the heat and blend until smooth and creamy using a stick blender
or in a food processor, adding a little extra stock if the soup is too thick. Season to taste
with salt and pepper, bearing in mind that the capers are quite salty.

To serve, ladle the soup into bowls and sprinkle over the reserved chickpeas, a few extra
capers and a little sumac.

Nutrition tip

You'll get a good boost of fibre from this soup, courtesy of the chickpeas.
And much of this fibre is the soluble kind that can help reduce cholesterol.

STIR IN a handful of baby spinach leaves at the same time as the chickpeas to add a fresh green element.
You could also serve the soup unblended.

SPRINKLE OVER a handful of grated Parmesan cheese or nutritional yeast flakes just before serving.

FOR A CURRIED CHICKPEA SOUP, leave out the capers and add your favourite curry powder,
to taste. Also, try replacing the stock with coconut milk to give a lovely creamy texture and flavour,
as well as complement the curry spices.

SUPER-GREENS SOUP

This very 'green' soup is high in plant protein from the kale, spinach and broccoli. It's also extremely alkaline and only lightly cooked so easier on the digestive system. A sprinkling of bee pollen and spirulina powder gives an extra superfood boost, and dehydrated herb or vegetable powder enhances the flavour.

SERVES 3-4

2 leeks, very finely chopped ❖ 2 celery sticks, finely chopped

½ head of broccoli, cut into small florets

3–4 stems of kale, tough stalks removed, and leaves torn into large pieces

4–6 asparagus spears, woody ends broken off, sliced into 2.5cm (1in) pieces

1 small handful of parsley, leaves only ❖ 1 small handful of mint, leaves only

800ml (1⅓ pints) hot Cooked Vegetable Stock (see page 15)

salt and pepper

TO SERVE

1 tablespoon bee pollen ❖ 1 teaspoon spirulina powder

1 teaspoon Dehydrated Herb or Vegetable Powder (see page 131)

Using a multi-tiered steamer, layer the vegetables starting with the ones that take the longest to cook closest to the water, so from the bottom up, start with leeks, then celery, broccoli, kale and finally the asparagus. Lightly steam the vegetables for 10–15 minutes until just cooked.

If you don't have a steamer, lightly cook the vegetables in simmering water until just tender.

Tip the vegetables into a high-speed blender or the bowl of a food processor, add the parsley, mint and stock and blitz to a smooth consistency. Season to taste with salt and pepper.

To serve, ladle the soup into bowls and sprinkle over the bee pollen, spirulina and dehydrated herb or vegetable powder.

Nutrition tip

Crammed full of folic acid, plus cell-protective antioxidants,
this really does live up to it's 'super' label health-wise.

FOR A MORE SUBSTANTIAL MEAL, add cooked potatoes, beans, lentils or quinoa.

SCATTER OVER a handful of protein-rich toasted nuts or seeds for added crunch.

SQUEEZE IN the juice of a lemon or grapefruit to add a citrus tang; the vitamin C from the citrus fruit will also aid the absorption of iron in the green veg.

SERVE the soup chilled instead of warm.

CONFETTI SOUP

You can make this soup using any clear soup, consommé or light vegetable broth. Try my Quick No-recipe Light Vegetable Stock (see page 16), or just a good shop-bought vegetable bouillon powder or cube. The trick is that you should be able to see the 'confetti' in the soup, all the way down to the ones that might have sunk to the bottom of the bowl.

SERVES 2-3

2–3 baby courgettes ❄ 3–4 baby sweetcorn, thinly sliced crossways

3–4 large radishes, cut into thin matchsticks

1 small root vegetable, such as carrot, beetroot or parsnip, cut into small dice

700ml (1¼ pints) Quick No-Recipe Light Vegetable Stock (see page 16) or vegetable bouillon, or clear soup

1 small handful of peas or sugar snap peas

1 small handful of delicate herbs, such as fennel, basil, dill and chives, finely chopped, plus extra to garnish

1 small handful of pomegranate seeds ❄ salt and pepper

Score the skin of the baby courgettes lengthways to make shallow, v-shaped grooves then slice very thinly crossways. Gently mix the courgettes with the sweetcorn, radishes and diced root vegetable of choice.

Gently heat the vegetable stock and stir in the confetti vegetable shapes, peas or sugar snaps, herbs and pomegranate seeds. Simmer for a few minutes to warm everything through then season to taste with salt and pepper.

To serve, ladle the broth into bowls and scatter over a few extra herbs

Nutrition tip

Despite being light on calories, this soup will fill you up and has a good content of potassium, which helps to maintain a healthy blood pressure.

YOU CAN MAKE 'confetti' out of any raw vegetables as long as you cut or slice them finely enough: very finely diced rainbow chard stems make beautiful multi-coloured sprinkles; shaved broccoli florets turn into tiny broccoli grains (this works well with purple-sprouting broccoli, cauliflower and bright green Romanesco, too); thinly sliced pink or purple radicchio form vibrant ribbons; or try a selection of tiny edible leaves and flowers scattered over the top.

FRESH TOMATO SOUP

This is almost like a fresh savoury smoothie and is completely raw. You can, of course, gently warm the soup – just don't heat it too much or cook it for too long, otherwise the soup loses its freshness and the tomatoes become watery.

SERVES 2-3

4–6 large ripe tomatoes, roughly chopped

2 red peppers, deseeded and roughly chopped

1–2 celery sticks, roughly chopped ❉ ½ onion, roughly chopped

½ red chilli pepper, deseeded and roughly chopped

½ small garlic clove, roughly chopped

1 small handful of parsley, roughly chopped

100ml (3½fl oz) Raw Vegetable Stock (see page 16) or water

1 small handful of basil leaves ❉ salt and pepper

Put the tomatoes, red peppers, celery, onion, chilli, garlic, parsley and stock or water in a high-speed blender or food processor and blitz to a finely chopped, soupy consistency. Add more water, or blend for longer, if you prefer a thinner soup. Season to taste with salt and pepper.

To serve, ladle the soup into bowls, or serve in chilled glasses, with a few basil leaves to garnish.

Nutrition tip

Even quite small amounts of parsley provide good amounts of vitamin K, which is important for normal blood clotting and strong bones.

BLEND in a handful of soaked cashews or the flesh of ⅓ avocado for a creamy soup. Serve as a dip with crudités.

BLEND for slightly longer to make a very smooth soup then serve as a salad dressing, or as a sauce for a raw main meal with spiralized courgettes or cucumber noodles.

ADD a dash of Tabasco or Worcestershire sauce and use as a base of a Bloody Mary.

SWISS CHARD & CELERY SOUP

Celery and the stems of Swiss chard are naturally high in sodium so you may find that you hardly need to add any salt to this soup.

SERVES 3-4

2 tbsp olive oil or coconut oil ❄ 1 red onion, finely chopped

4–5 celery sticks, finely chopped, leaves reserved

3–4 garlic cloves, peeled and left whole

1 large bunch of Swiss chard, stems finely chopped
and leaves torn into large pieces

1 small rosemary sprig, needles finely chopped

1 small bunch of parsley, leaves only

600ml (20fl oz) hot Cooked Vegetable Stock (see page 15)

salt and pepper

Heat the oil in a large saucepan, add the onion, celery, garlic, chard stems and rosemary and fry gently until the vegetables have softened.

Stir in the chard leaves, parsley and stock and simmer for 5–10 minutes until the chard leaves are tender.

Remove the pan from the heat, blend the soup to a rough purée using a stick blender or in a food processor. Season to taste with salt and pepper.

To serve, ladle the soup into bowls and sprinkle over a few celery leaves to garnish.

Nutrition tip

Nutritious and hydrating, this is a slimline soup. Swiss chard is a source of anaemia-protective iron and the antioxidant vitamin E.

CRUMBLED crispy bacon adds an extra savoury flavour.

STIR IN a handful of cooked beans, such as cannellini, haricot or butter beans for a more filling dish with added fibre.

ADD A DOLLOP of a spicy tomato salsa or red pepper pesto.

SOUPY SALAD

The soup part is simply juiced vegetables, which you can gently warm up if you prefer, while the salad part is similar to coleslaw, made with shredded and grated raw vegetables. The salad adds texture and body to the soup, as do a few chopped or ground nuts and seeds. It might not sound promising as a dish, but I assure you it's really tasty and leaves you feeling full, yet still light.

SERVES 3-4

FOR THE SOUP

3–4 large carrots, chopped into chunks ❖ 4 large tomatoes, chopped into large chunks

2–3 celery sticks, chopped into chunks

1 lemon grass stalk, outer layer removed, and chopped into small pieces

1 small handful of basil leaves ❖ 1 garlic clove, peeled, and left whole

salt and pepper ❖ mixed nuts and seeds, chopped, to serve (optional)

FOR THE SALAD

2 large carrots, coarsely grated ❖ 2 celery sticks, finely chopped, leaves reserved to garnish

2 small Baby Gem lettuces, finely shredded ❖ 1 raw beetroot, scrubbed and coarsely grated

1 small bunch of parsley, finely chopped

To make the soup, run all the ingredients through a juicer. Season to taste with salt and pepper and chill in the fridge for 2–3 hours, or until ready to serve.

For the salad, mix together all the ingredients.

To serve, place a large spoonful of the salad into each serving bowl, then pour over the soup. Scatter the chopped nuts and seeds over the top, if desired, and add a few chopped celery leaves.

Nutrition tip

There's a lot of beta-carotene in this soup, which can be turned into vitamin A. It's great for keeping your immune system healthy.

JUICE any savoury-flavoured fruits or vegetables to make the soup and add a pinch of ground spices, if you want to turn up the heat.

MAKE the salad part using any finely shredded or chopped raw fruits or vegetables, and add a little chopped dried fruit for a chewy sweetness.

SWAP things around and serve the salad with some of the soup spooned over as a dressing.

LOOKING to break the monotony of a juice cleanse? This is a great soup to turn to.

SWEET POTATO & PEAR SOUP

This delicate soup can be served warm or chilled, but for a more intense, robust flavour, roast the sweet potatoes and pears before blending.

SERVES 4-6

2 tbsp vegan butter ❋ 1 onion, finely chopped

3 large sweet potatoes, peeled and cut into small chunks

2–3 large ripe pears, cut into large chunks,
plus extra finely chopped to garnish

600ml (20fl oz) hot Quick No-Recipe Light Vegetable Stock (see page 16)

3–4 tbsp Macadamia Cream Cheese (see page 137) or any dairy or vegan cream cheese alternative

salt and pepper

Melt the butter in a large saucepan, add the onion and fry gently until softened. Add the sweet potatoes and pears and sauté for a few minutes.

Pour in the stock and simmer for 15–20 minutes until the sweet potatoes are tender, then stir in the cream cheese.

Remove the pan from the heat and blend until smooth using a stick blender or in a food processor. Season to taste with salt and pepper.

To serve, ladle the soup into teacups or small bowls and top with a little chopped pear.

Nutrition tip

Sweet potatoes have a healthily low GI, keeping your blood sugar steady. Plus they're a good source of vitamin A, which is important for the immune system.

❋

CRUMBLE a little blue cheese or goats' cheese over the top – the flavours go together beautifully.

SCATTER over a few toasted flaked almonds, or shards of crispy pancetta or smoky bacon for added crunch.

GARNISH with a few edible flowers for a pretty finishing touch.

IF SERVING CHILLED, a little splash of eau de vie, such as Poire William, gives a nice boozy finish.

CHUNKY BORLOTTI BEAN & KALE SOUP

I've used cooked dried borlotti beans in this chunky soup, but you could use canned borlotti instead to save time. The kale could also be substituted for cavolo nero or Savoy cabbage in this rustic, Italian-style soup.

SERVES 3-4

300g (10½oz) dried borlotti beans, rinsed and drained

2 tbsp olive oil or coconut oil ❄ 1 red onion, finely chopped

1 carrot, finely chopped ❄ 1 celery stick, finely chopped

2–3 garlic cloves, finely chopped

2 small red chillies, deseeded and finely chopped, plus extra to garnish

1 tsp fennel seeds ❄ 4–6 large ripe tomatoes, roughly chopped

4–5 kale leaves, stems removed and leaves chopped into large pieces

1 small handful of parsley leaves, roughly chopped

450ml (16fl oz) hot Cooked Vegetable Stock (see page 15) ❄ salt and pepper

Put the beans in a bowl, cover with plenty of cold water and leave to soak overnight, then drain.

Place the beans in a large saucepan and cover with fresh cold water. Bring to the boil, then turn the heat down and simmer for about 1 hour, or until tender. Drain the beans and set aside until ready to use.

Heat the oil in a large saucepan, add the onion, carrot, celery, garlic, chilli and fennel seeds and cook gently until the vegetables have softened.

Add the cooked beans, tomatoes, kale, reserving a little to garnish, parsley and stock and simmer for 10–15 minutes until the vegetables are cooked and the tomatoes tender.

Remove the pan from the heat and part-blend the soup using a stick blender, or in a food processor if you want a thick, creamy consistency, or leave the soup unblended for a more rustic, chunky texture. Season to taste with salt and pepper.

To serve, ladle the soup into bowls and sprinkle over a little chopped red chilli and the reserved kale.

Nutrition tip

Kale provides lutein, an antioxidant that is believed to be good for protecting your eyes.

SERVE with crusty rustic bread, or stir in a handful of cooked pasta for a more substantial minestrone-style soup.

ADD spicy cured sausage or salami, crispy pancetta or cooked ham.

A HANDFUL of grated Parmesan cheese and a few torn basil leaves complement the flavours of the soup.

BROCCOLI & LEMON SOUP

This soup is a great way of using the whole broccoli, stalk and all. The lemon balances the slightly sulphurous taste that cooked broccoli can sometimes have, while the sriracha sauce gives the soup a sweet-spicy finish.

SERVES 3-4

1–2 tbsp olive oil ✳ 1 onion, finely chopped

1–2 garlic cloves, finely chopped ✳ 2–3 celery sticks, roughly chopped

1 head of broccoli, broken into small florets, stalk reserved

600ml (20fl oz) hot Cooked Vegetable Stock (see page 15)

juice and finely grated zest of 1 lemon, plus extra lemon slices
to garnish ✳ 1 small red chilli, deseeded and finely chopped

1 small handful of basil leaves ✳ salt and pepper

Sriracha Sauce (see page 135), to serve

Heat half of the oil in a large saucepan, add the onion, garlic and celery
and fry gently until softened but not coloured.

Add the broccoli florets and stock and simmer for 10–15 minutes until the broccoli is tender.
Add the lemon juice and zest.

While the soup is cooking, peel the broccoli stalk and slice it very finely crossways
(a mandoline is ideal for this). Toss the sliced broccoli stalk with the chilli and
salt and pepper and dress with the remaining olive oil.

The soup should now be ready, remove the pan from the heat and blend the soup
to a silky smooth consistency using a stick blender or in a food processor.
Season to taste with salt and pepper.

To serve, ladle the soup into bowls, scatter over the sliced broccoli stalks and
basil leaves and top with lemon slices and a drizzle of sriracha.

Nutrition tip

Broccoli is a really good source of folic acid, essential for making red blood cells.
The vitamin is also essential prior to and in the early stages of pregnancy.

✳

CRUMBLE goats' cheese, ricotta or blue cheese over the soup.

TRY fresh mint instead of lemon as a flavouring.

THIS SOUP is also lovely chilled with maybe a little diced cucumber mixed
in to give freshness and texture.

USE lemon oil instead of olive oil to dress the broccoli stalk garnish.

PUMPKIN SOUP

Pumpkin, like other squash, is delicious roasted when it becomes sweet and rich.
The curry spices complement the pumpkin and give an extra warming flavour.
Keep the seeds from the pumpkin, clean to remove any fibres, then roast
and scatter over the soup before serving.

SERVES 3-4

1 medium pumpkin, cut in half, deseeded (keep the seeds for roasting),
peeled and cut into large chunks

1 large onion, roughly chopped ❊ 2–3 tbsp olive oil or melted coconut oil

2 tsp garam masala ❊ 800ml (1⅓ pints) hot Cooked Vegetable Stock (see page 15)

salt and pepper

TO SERVE

2– 3 tbsp Raw Cashew Cream (see page 138) ❊ 2–3 tbsp Popped Savoury Quinoa (see page 130)

2–3 tbsp Roasted Pumpkin Seeds (see page 130)

Preheat the oven to 190°C (375°F) Gas Mark 5.

Mix the pumpkin and onion with the oil and garam masala in a large bowl until combined,
then tip into a large roasting tray. Spread the veg out in an even layer and roast for 30–40
minutes until the pumpkin is golden and cooked through.

Tip the roasted pumpkin and onion into the bowl of a food processor with the stock and
blend until silky smooth. Season to taste with salt and pepper.

To serve, ladle the soup into mugs or bowls and serve topped with a swirl of cashew cream
and a sprinkling of popped quinoa and roasted pumpkin seeds.

Nutrition tip

The orange colour of pumpkin signifies that it's a great source of carotenoids –
antioxidants that help protect cells against damaging free radicals.

SERVE TOPPED with nutritional yeast flakes or grated cheese and big chunks of rustic bread for dunking.

POUR INTO a hollowed-out pumpkin or squash shell for a fun way to serve the soup at a Halloween or
autumn party.

ADD coconut milk or coconut cream for an extra rich, creamy finish, or blend in a couple of tablespoons
of almond butter or peanut butter for added protein.

LEEK & POTATO SOUP

Vichyssoise is a classic soup that's lovely served warm or chilled. Use a firm-fleshed or waxy variety of potato, such as Yukon Gold, Charlotte or Anya to give a good flavour and creamy texture.

SERVES 3-4

2–3 large white potatoes, scrubbed and finely diced ❄ 2–3 tbsp vegan butter

3–4 large leeks, roughly chopped, plus extra finely sliced to garnish

1 large onion, finely chopped ❄ 400ml (14fl oz) hot Cooked Vegetable Stock (see page 15)

pinch of freshly grated nutmeg

100ml (3½fl oz) Raw Cashew Cream (see page 138) or any dairy or vegan cream alternative

salt and pepper ❄ favourite crackers, to serve

Cook the potatoes in a saucepan of boiling salted water until tender, then drain.

While the potatoes are cooking, heat the butter in a separate large pan, add the leeks and onion and sauté gently for 3-4 minutes until starting to soften.

Add the stock and simmer for 5–10 minutes until the leeks and onion are tender. Add the cooked potatoes, nutmeg and season to taste with salt and pepper.

Remove the pan from the heat and blend to a silky smooth consistency using a stick blender or in a food processor. Stir in the cream just before serving and heat through, if you like. If serving chilled, there is no need to warm the soup.

To serve, ladle the soup into bowls and scatter over the finely sliced leeks and crackers as a garnish.

Nutrition tip

Leeks are high in a fibre called inulin, which stimulates the growth of beneficial gut bacteria and helps keep your intestines healthy.

THIN THE SOUP with extra stock or water so it's easily sippable from a cup or glass, especially if serving chilled.

NATURAL YOGURT gives a lighter-tasting soup instead of the cream.

ADD a couple of chopped courgettes to boost the green vegetable content.

CARROT, ORANGE & CORIANDER SOUP

The flavours of orange, coriander and parsley have a natural affinity with carrot, and make this soup both comforting and fresh-tasting at the same time.

SERVES 4-6

1 tbsp olive oil or coconut oil

1 large onion, finely chopped ❋ 4–5 large carrots, grated

600ml (20fl oz) hot Cooked Vegetable Stock (see page 15)

1 small bunch of parsley, leaves only

1 small bunch of coriander, leaves only, plus extra to garnish

juice and finely grated zest of 1 large orange ❋ salt and pepper

Heat the oil in a large saucepan, add the onion and sauté gently until lightly golden.

Add the carrots and stock and simmer for 10–15 minutes until softened.

Add the parsley leaves, coriander leaves, orange juice and zest and blend to a smooth purée using a stick blender or in a food processor, adding extra stock if you prefer a soup with a thinner consistency. Season to taste with salt and pepper.

To serve, ladle the soup into bowls and top with a little extra chopped coriander leaves.

Nutrition tip

You'll get all of your recommended daily allowance of vitamin A – important for the health of the immune system and skin – from this carroty soup.

❋

FOR A SPICY SOUP, add ½ teaspoon crushed coriander or cumin seeds to the onion before sautéing.

ADD a handful of grated carrot to give texture as well as extra nutrients and fibre.

IF YOU'RE USING organic carrots, chop a few of the fronds to sprinkle over the top.

ALKALIZING GREEN SOUP

This raw soup is wonderfully detoxifying and tastes delicious.
I first saw a version of this soup in an amazing organic co-op
in San Francisco called Rainbow Grocery and was compelled
to make my own version when I got home.

SERVES 4-6

1 large cucumber, roughly chopped

2–3 courgettes, roughly chopped

1 large ripe avocado, cut in half, stone removed and flesh scooped out

150g (5½oz) sugar snap peas, roughly chopped

1 small bunch of kale, tough stalks removed

1 small bunch of parsley, leaves only

1 small bunch of coriander, leaves only

Juice and finely grated zest of 1 lemon

2.5cm (1in) piece fresh root ginger, peeled

300ml (10fl oz) filtered water ❋ salt and pepper

Place all the ingredients in a high-speed blender and blend until silky
smooth. If the consistency is too thick, blend with a little more water.
Chill for 2–3 hours, or until ready to eat, or blend with a handful of ice
if you want to eat the soup straightaway.

To serve, pour the soup into chilled glasses or bowls.

Nutrition tip

This raw soup is high in iron and vitamin C, and is totally alkaline –
great as one of the dishes to eat following a juice cleanse.

HEAT the soup gently to 45°C (113°F) if you want to eat it warm,
but still keep it 'raw'.

TOP with a spoonful of Gazpacho Salsa (see page 135),
or a dollop of raw almond cream.

CRAVE a bit of crunch? Serve with dehydrated veggie crisps or crackers.

GOLDEN BUTTERNUT SQUASH SOUP

This golden-hued soup is so thick and filling it makes a hearty main meal.
Sweet potatoes, pumpkin or any other seasonal squash can be used instead
of the butternut squash.

SERVES 2-3

3 large butternut squash, cut in half lengthways and deseeded ❊ 2–3 tbsp olive oil

1 red pepper, deseeded and cut into chunks ❊ 1 large onion, finely chopped

1 large carrot, thinly sliced ❊ 1 celery stick, thinly sliced ❊ 3 garlic cloves, thinly sliced

30g (1oz) plain flour ❊ 600ml (20fl oz) hot Cooked Vegetable Stock (see page 15)

400g (14oz) can chopped tomatoes ❊ large pinch of dried chilli flakes

1 tsp chopped thyme leaves ❊ salt and pepper

TO SERVE

Spiced Parsnip Crisps (see page 134) ❊ Cajun spice mix

Sriracha Sauce (see page 135) ❊ Macadamia Cream Cheese (see page 137)

Preheat the oven to 160°C (325°F) Gas Mark 3.

Place the squash on a roasting tray and drizzle over 1 tablespoon of the oil.
Season with salt and pepper and toss until combined. Roast the squash for 1 hour,
or until tender and slightly caramelized. Leave to cool slightly, then scoop the
squash out of the skins and purée it in a blender.

Heat the remaining oil in a saucepan, add the red pepper, onion, carrot, celery
and garlic and fry gently until softened.

Remove the pan from the heat, add the flour and stir well. Gradually add the stock, stirring
constantly, and then stir in the puréed squash, tomatoes and chilli flakes.

Return the pan to the heat and simmer for 20 minutes until warmed through and thickened,
adding extra stock to thin the soup if necessary. Add the thyme and check the seasoning.

To serve, ladle the soup into bowls and serve sprinkled with the parsnip crisps and Cajun
spice mix. Finish with a drizzle of sriracha and macadamia cream cheese.

Nutrition tip

Red and orange veg provide a wealth of carotenoid and flavonoids, which have antioxidant and
anti-inflammatory effects. With a healthy dose or quercetin-rich garlic and onions, this soup
could help damp down minor allergies too.

SPRINKLE with crispy smoked pancetta and grated Parmesan cheese,
or try nutritional yeast flakes for a vegan alternative.

WATERMELON GAZPACHO

Serve this pretty, sweet and spicy gazpacho as a summer
starter. It also makes a super-refreshing drink on its own,
a bit like watermelon limeade, or the base of a cocktail.

SERVES 4-6

juice of 3 limes, skin removed, and fruit cut into chunks, seeds removed

1 large cucumber, chopped into large chunks

2–3 large red peppers, deseeded and roughly chopped

½ small red chilli or jalapeño pepper, deseeded and roughly chopped

1 medium watermelon ❊ slices of lime and cucumber, to garnish

Run the lime, cucumber, red peppers and chilli through a juicer.

Cut the rind from the watermelon and cut into large chunks,
removing the seeds as you go. Place in a high-speed blender with the
juiced fruit and vegetables and blend until smooth.

To serve, half-fill chilled glasses with ice, pour over the gazpacho, then
garnish each serving with a twist of cucumber and a slice of lime.

Nutrition tip

This slimline soup will hydrate you and is a good source of the antioxidant
lycopene, which has been linked with good cardiovascular health.

FREEZE in ice-cube trays and use as flavoured ice in drinks or chilled soups or
freeze into ice pops, sorbet or granita.

A SHOT of vodka turns the soup into a vibrant summer cocktail.

TOMATO CAULI RICE SOUP

This is a simple raw soup made from a savoury juice that can be warmed gently if you don't like the thought of eating it cold. The 'riced' courgette and cauliflower add a bit of texture – a welcome addition if you're midway through a juice cleanse.

SERVES 3-4

½ head of cauliflower, outer leaves removed, broken into florets

1 large courgette, roughly chopped

6–8 large ripe tomatoes, roughly chopped

2 large red peppers, deseeded and finely chopped

2 large carrots, roughly chopped ✳ 2 celery sticks, roughly chopped

½ red onion, roughly chopped ✳ ½ garlic clove, peeled

salt and pepper

Place the cauliflower and courgette in the bowl of a food processor and blitz into rice-like grains. Tip out onto kitchen paper to absorb any excess moisture.

Run the rest of the ingredients through a juicer and season to taste with salt and pepper.

To serve, place a couple of spoons of the veggie rice into bowls and ladle over the savoury juice.

Nutrition tip

Cauliflower is part of the cruciferous family of vegetables, which has been linked with lower risk of some cancers.

✳

HEAT the soup gently to 45°C (113°F) if you want to eat it warm, but still keep it 'raw'.

STIR-FRY the cauliflower and courgette 'rice' and spoon a little of the warmed juice over to make an interesting side dish.

STIR IN shredded carrot or finely diced red pepper for extra raw-veggie texture.

ASPARAGUS & FENNEL SOUP

This light, delicate soup is good served warm or chilled and is at its best when asparagus is in season and plentiful.

SERVES 3-4

10–12 asparagus spears, woody ends broken off

1 large fennel bulb, roughly chopped, fronds reserved

3–4 spring onions, coarsely chopped

400ml (14fl oz) hot Cooked Vegetable Stock (see page 15)

juice and finely grated zest of 1 lemon　*　salt and pepper

1 small rosemary sprig, needles very finely chopped, to garnish

Set aside 2 asparagus spears and roughly chop the remaining ones. Place the asparagus, fennel, spring onions and stock in a large saucepan and simmer for 20-25 minutes until the vegetables are tender. You can also sauté the vegetables briefly in a little oil before adding the stock, but this will result in a slightly darker-coloured soup.

Remove the pan from the heat and purée the soup until smooth using a stick blender or in a high-speed blender, adding more stock if necessary. Add the lemon juice and zest and season to taste with salt and pepper.

Cut the reserved asparagus spears into fine discs or shave into long ribbons with a vegetable peeler.

To serve, ladle the soup into bowls and serve with the reserved fennel fronds, rosemary and discs or ribbons of raw asparagus scattered over the top.

Nutrition tip

There's no vegetable richer in folic acid – needed for manufacturing red blood cells – than fresh asparagus. This soup is also good for your digestive system, with soothing fennel and prebiotic fibre.

SERVE chilled on a hot day, topped with a swirl of soured cream and a few ice cubes.

FRESH MINT, tarragon or dill would all be good substitutes for the rosemary.

COOK slices of Parma ham or prosciutto in a dry frying pan until crisp then crumble over the top for a savoury meaty garnish.

CARROT, COUSCOUS & CHARD SOUP

I've used giant couscous as the larger grains are more robust in this rustic soup-cum-stew, although the standard couscous works, too, just be careful not to overcook it. I sauté the carrot ribbons briefly to keep an element of crunch, but you could cook them for longer and then blend all the cooked vegetables together and serve the couscous stirred in at the end.

SERVES 3-4

200g (7oz) giant couscous ❋ 650ml (22fl oz) hot Cooked Vegetable Stock (see page 15)

2 tbsp olive oil or coconut oil ❋ 2 tsp Dukkah (see page 128), plus extra for sprinkling

1 large onion, roughly chopped ❋ 2 celery sticks, coarsely chopped

2 garlic cloves, finely chopped

1 large bunch of rainbow chard, stems and leaves separated, and roughly chopped

2–3 large carrots, preferably purple, sliced with a vegetable peeler into thin ribbons

Pour the couscous into a large saucepan and lightly toast the grains over a medium-high heat, stirring often. Pour in the stock, stir and simmer for 10–15 minutes until the couscous is cooked through. Take the pan off the heat and leave to one side.

While the couscous is cooking, heat the oil in a large sauté pan, add the dukkah, onion, celery, garlic and chard stems and sauté gently until softened.

Add the chard leaves and carrots and cook gently until softened slightly and the chard leaves have wilted. Add them to the pan with the couscous and stock and simmer briefly until heated through.

To serve, ladle the soup into bowls and serve with a little extra dukkah sprinkled over the top.

Nutrition tip

This soup provides a healthy balance of vegetables and carbohydrates – serve with cheese or spicy sausage as suggested to turn it into a completely balanced meal.

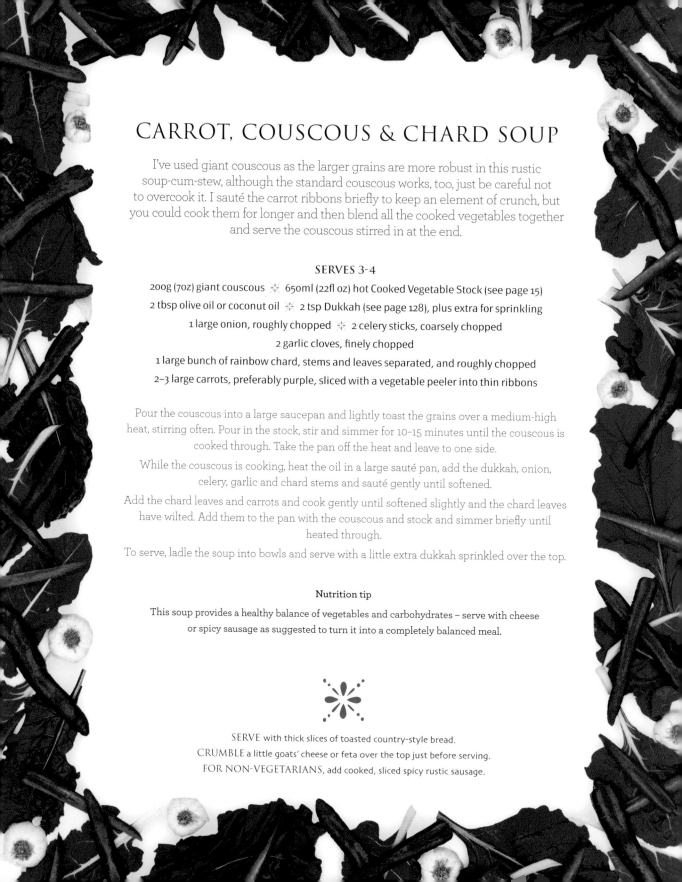

SERVE with thick slices of toasted country-style bread.
CRUMBLE a little goats' cheese or feta over the top just before serving.
FOR NON-VEGETARIANS, add cooked, sliced spicy rustic sausage.

BEET & BARBERRY SOUP

The sweetness of the beetroot in this soup is tempered by the sour flavour of the dried barberries and the spiciness of the horseradish cream. Barberries are small red berries that are often used in Iranian cooking, and add a slight sharpness to the flavour. Dried unsweetened cranberries make a good substitute. Serve warm or chilled.

SERVES 3-4

4–5 large raw beetroots with leaves, stalks and leaves removed and reserved, to garnish
400ml (14fl oz) hot Cooked Vegetable Stock (see page 15) ❋ 2 tbsp dried barberries
squeeze of lemon juice (optional) ❋ salt and pepper

TO SERVE

½ tsp grated fresh horseradish
3 tbsp Raw Almond Yogurt (see page 137) or Raw Cashew Cream (see page 138)
2 tbsp flaked almonds
wheat crackers or lightly toasted rye bread

Place the beetroots in a large saucepan of boiling salted water and cook, uncovered, for about 30–40 minutes until tender. Remove the beetroots and set aside until cool enough to handle. When cool, peel off the skins (wearing rubber gloves is advisable) and chop the flesh into large chunks.

Using a stick blender or high-speed blender, purée the cooked beetroots with the stock and half the barberries until a thick, smooth consistency. Season to taste with salt and pepper, and add a squeeze of lemon juice if the soup is too sweet.

Before serving, mix the horseradish with the yogurt or cream. Toast the flaked almonds in a dry frying pan for 3-4 minutes until lightly golden. Finely chop the reserved beetroot leaves.

To serve, ladle the soup into bowls and top with a spoonful of the horseradish cream, beetroot leaves, flaked almonds and the remaining barberries. Serve with a few wheat crackers or lightly toasted rye bread, if you like.

Nutrition tip

Beetroots are naturally rich in nitrates, which the body uses to make the nitric oxide that can lower blood pressure and optimize physical performance.

FLAKED cooked salmon, smoked trout or mackerel, or slices of gravadlax make a delicious fishy topping.
DICED hard-boiled eggs or some salty feta or goats' cheese all team well with cooked beetroot.
INSTEAD OF the beetroot leaves, use chopped chives or watercress as a green garnish.
USE any leftover beetroot stems and leaves in a salad, or sauté the leaves like spinach, or juice them – just don't throw them away as they're full of goodness.

COURGETTI KALE SOUP

The spiralized courgette adds a great textural element to this soup. I only partially cooked it so it's still al dente (cooking courgetti for too long makes it limp and watery) but you could blitz the whole lot together to make a smooth blended soup. The sautéed cavolo nero gives a savoury 'meaty' flavour to the dish and the toasted pine nuts add crunch.

SERVES 3-4

2–3 courgettes, spiralized or cut into julienne strips ❋ 1 tbsp olive oil or coconut oil

4–5 cavolo nero leaves, or the equivalent amount of kale, stalks removed and leaves torn into large pieces

600ml (20fl oz) Passata (see page 138) or Three Tomato Soup (see page 86)

pinch of sumac ❋ salt and pepper

3–4 tbsp toasted pine nuts, to serve

Blanch the courgetti briefly in boiling water until just softened, then drain and place on kitchen paper until required.

Heat the oil in a large sauté pan, add the cavolo nero and sauté until wilted and softened.

Pour the passata into a saucepan and heat gently. Add the courgetti and cavolo nero and heat until warmed through. Season to taste with salt and pepper.

To serve, ladle the soup into bowls, add a pinch of sumac to each one and scatter over the pine nuts.

Nutrition tip

Kale is super-rich in vitamin C and lutein (good for eyes), while courgettes provides potassium, folic acid and vitamin A.

SCATTER over a handful of grated Parmesan cheese just before serving.
CHOPPED sun-dried tomatoes add an extra-rich tomatoey flavour.
SAUTÉED cubes of pancetta or chorizo work well with the tomato-based soup.
STIR IN barbecued prawns or chicken.

RAW AVOCADO & CUCUMBER SOUP

This raw soup is really refreshing on a hot day, and the chives give a gentle oniony flavour without being too overpowering. The chilled cucumber pearls are a pretty garnish but if you don't have a mini melon baller, or the time or patience to make them, dice the cucumber instead – it'll taste just the same!

SERVES 3-4

2 large ripe avocados, cut in half, stones removed and flesh scooped out

2 large cucumbers, peeled if not organic, and roughly chopped

juice of 1 lemon ✳ 100ml (3½fl oz) cold water

1 small bunch of chives, snipped ✳ salt and pepper

TO SERVE

1 cucumber, cut in half lengthways

½ avocado, stone removed, peeled and diced

Place all the ingredients, except the garnish and reserving a few chives to garnish, in a high-speed blender and blitz until silky smooth – you may need to add a little extra water, depending on how juicy your cucumbers are. Season to taste with salt and pepper.

Before serving, make the cucumber pearls. Using a mini melon baller, scoop out small balls of cucumber, avoiding the seedy part running down the middle. (Save any leftover cucumber to use in a juice or chop into a salad.)

To serve, ladle the soup into chilled bowls or glasses and top with the diced avocado, cucumber pearls and the reserved chives.

Nutrition tip

Avocados provide good monunsaturated fats, which are the type that reduce cholesterol. They're also a really good source of vitamin E and some B vitamins.

A HANDFUL of chopped tomatoes gives an additional savoury flavour.

BLEND in a few sprigs of fresh coriander for a herbal boost.

FREEZE the blended soup to make a savoury ice cream, and serve in scoops in chilled bowls or glasses.

GAZPACHO

This chilled soup is really easy and is best made in the summer when tomatoes are at their best and most flavoursome. Some gazpacho recipes call for the addition of stale bread, but I prefer to keep my version simply fresh fruit and vegetables. Serve it with a crunchy salsa topping to add texture to this otherwise smooth soup – what's more, the salsa can be made out of the same ingredients as the soup.

SERVES 3-4

1 cucumber, roughly chopped

500g (1lb 2oz) ripe tomatoes, roughly chopped

1 red pepper, deseeded and roughly chopped

3 celery sticks, roughly chopped ❉ 3–4 spring onions, roughly chopped

2 small garlic cloves, roughly chopped

1 small handful of parsley or basil leaves

1 tbsp olive oil, plus extra for drizzling ❉ 100ml (3½fl oz) water

salt and pepper ❉ Gazpacho Salsa, to serve (see page 135)

Place all the ingredients in a high-speed blender, then blend until smooth, adding a little extra water if needed. Season to taste with salt and pepper.

Cover the soup and chill in the fridge for 2–3 hours, or until ready to serve.

To serve, ladle the soup into bowls and top with the gazpacho salsa and an extra drizzle of olive oil.

Nutrition tip

The tomatoes in gazpacho give you a great boost of lycopene – as well as being cardio-protective this antioxidant may offer some protection for skin against UV damage.

❉

IF PREFERRED, serve the soup warm: heat gently but don't over-heat as it will turn watery and lose its fresh flavour.

FOR A bloody Mary-type twist, add a couple of shots of good vodka.

A PINCH of hot paprika or a few drops of Worcestershire sauce or Tabasco would give a spicy hit.

BUTTERNUT NOODLE SOUP

I like this veggie-dense soup served chunky so it's more like a stew but you can also blend the green vegetables into a sauce to serve over the butternut squash noodles. I've caramelized the onions to give a crispy, sweet finish and added a pinch of panch phoran (an Indian whole spice mix) for a hint of curry flavour.

SERVES 3-4

2 tablespoons olive oil or coconut oil ❋ 2 red onions, very finely sliced

1 teaspoon sugar or maple syrup, or sweetener of choice

pinch of Panch Phoran (see page 128) ❋ 2 garlic cloves, finely chopped

1 leek, finely chopped ❋ 2 large courgettes, diced into small cubes

4–5 cavolo nero leaves or the equivalent of kale, stalks removed
and leaves torn into large pieces

3–4 spring onions, finely chopped ❋ 600ml (20fl oz) hot Cooked Vegetable Stock (see page 15)

1 large butternut squash, peeled and spiralized, or cut into julienne strips

1 small handful of parsley leaves, roughly chopped ❋ salt and pepper

First caramelize the red onions. Heat 1 tablespoon of the oil in a large sauté pan, add the onions, sugar and a pinch of salt and cook, stirring frequently, over a medium-high heat for 10 minutes, or until the onions are cooked, crisp and golden. Tip out of the pan onto kitchen paper and set aside.

Heat the remaining oil in the sauté pan or a saucepan, add the panch phoran and cook briefly until the spices release their fragrance and start to pop.

Add the garlic, leek and courgettes and sauté gently until the vegetables soften. Add the cavolo nero and spring onions and cook for a further 5 minutes until wilted and softened.

Pour in the stock and add the butternut squash, cover, and simmer for 5–10 minutes until the 'noodles' are tender. Stir in the parsley and season to taste with salt and pepper.

To serve, ladle the soup into bowls and scatter the caramelized onions over the top.

Nutrition tip

Orange-hued butternut squash provides lots of carotenoid antioxidants. If you're keeping an eye on your weight, it's more waistline-friendly than sweet potato.

A COUPLE of softly poached or fried eggs on top make a more substantial meal.
ADD cooked flaked white fish or salmon for extra protein, or sprinkle with toasted nuts and seeds.
TURN the 'noodles' into a type of rosti instead of a soup, and serve with the greens on top.

HIDDEN VEG SOUP

Adding raw grated veg is an easy way to bulk out a cooked meal as well as give it texture. It's also a good option if you want to disguise vegetables from veg-haters, young or old! I've used little star-shaped pasta, stelline, as it cooks quite quickly, while ready-made passata makes a convenient base and speeds up the preparation time, too. I often add lemon juice or zest to tomato-based sauces and soups to give a brightness and freshness of flavour, and a pinch of sumac has a similar effect.

SERVES 3-4

100–125g (3½–4½oz) dried pasta, such as stelline, orzo, trofie or short-cut macaroni

500ml (18fl oz) passata ❖ 1 large courgette, coarsely grated

1 large carrot, coarsely grated

1 small handful of mixed herbs, such as basil, parsley, thyme,
oregano and marjoram, finely chopped

few pinches of sumac ❖ salt and pepper

Cook the dried pasta following the packet instructions, then drain and set aside.

While the pasta is cooking, pour the passata into a large saucepan and add the grated courgette and carrot, then simmer for 5–10 minutes until the vegetables have softened but are still al dente.

Stir in the herbs, cooked pasta and season to taste with salt and pepper,
then simmer for a few more minutes until heated through.

To serve, ladle the soup into bowls and sprinkle over a pinch of sumac.

Nutrition tip

Fresh herbs bump up the health value of any dish – adding antioxidants, vitamin K and vitamin C.

BEETROOT, sweet potato, parsnip or red pepper also work well in this soup.

INCLUDE cubes of cooked ham or marinated tofu for added protein.

A HANDFUL of grated Parmesan cheese and/or a dollop of pesto make great toppings.

STIR IN a spoonful of Raw Cashew Cream (see page 138), cream or crème fraîche for a rich, creamy-textured soup.

MIXED MUSHROOM SOUP

I've used a combination of different mushrooms, including chestnut and fresh wild morels – although you could also use cultivated ones. They have a rich, earthy taste and a few wild mushrooms always go a long way flavour-wise.

SERVES 3-4

2 tbsp olive oil ✳ 1 onion, finely chopped

1 leek, finely chopped ✳ 2 garlic cloves, finely chopped

500g (1lb 2oz) mixed mushrooms, cleaned and roughly chopped, plus extra to serve

600ml (20fl oz) hot Cooked Vegetable Stock (see page 15)

2–3 thyme sprigs, leaves stripped ✳ 1 bay leaf

3 tbsp Raw Cashew Cream (see page 138) or crème fraîche

salt and pepper

Heat the oil in a large saucepan, add the onion, leek and garlic and sauté gently until softened.

Add the mushrooms and some salt and pepper and cook for 5–10 minutes until tender. Add the stock, thyme and bay leaf and simmer for 30 minutes.

Remove the pan from the heat, take out the bay leaf and stir in the cashew cream. Blend the soup until smooth and creamy using a stick blender, then check the seasoning and add more salt or pepper, if needed.

To serve, ladle the soup into bowls and scatter a few finely sliced fresh mushrooms over the top

Nutrition tip

Mushrooms are a good source of B vitamins that help our cells release energy from food. Pop them gill side up on a sunny windowsill before using and they'll be a good source vitamin D, too.

✳

TRY ADDING a small handful of soaked dried mushrooms, such as porcini, for an extra mushroomy flavour boost.

ADD A handful of cooked barley, brown rice or lentils for a hearty rustic meal.

A GLUG of Marsala wine adds a rich, luxuriant touch to this soup.

SPRING VEG SOUP

This soup can be made with any new-season spring vegetables. I've used wild garlic as it grows in profusion where I live, and also monk's beard (also known as agretti) as I love its fresh minerally taste and crisp succulent texture. It looks similar to chives, but its overriding flavour is similar to a combination of samphire, asparagus and spinach, all of which can be used as substitutions.

To minimize washing up, this soup can be made in a tiered steamer: the potatoes cooked in the vegetable stock in the base, and the green veg steamed above.

SERVES 2-3

250g (9oz) baby new potatoes, cut in half

4–5 wild garlic leaves, plus flowers to garnish, or 2 garlic cloves, peeled and left whole

600ml (20fl oz) hot Cooked Vegetable Stock (see page 15)

½ large head of broccoli, broken into small florets

2 large handfuls of monk's beard, samphire, baby spinach leaves or
asparagus spears, woody ends broken off

salt and pepper ❊ Fresh Herb Pesto (see page 135), to serve

Place the new potatoes and garlic cloves, if using instead of wild garlic, in a saucepan or in the base of a tiered steamer and pour over the stock. Bring to a simmer and place the broccoli and monk's beard in the steamer baskets above; the monk's beard will take the least time to cook so put this on the top. Steam the green vegetables until they're just cooked and simmer the potatoes until they're tender.

(If you don't have a steamer, boil the potatoes and garlic and cook the broccoli in a separate pan for 4–5 minutes, and the monk's beard in a third pan for 2–3 minutes.)

Remove half of the potatoes from the stock and set aside. Tip the broccoli into the pan with the remaining potatoes and the wild garlic, if using instead of the whole cloves, and blitz with a stick blender to make a finely textured soup. (Alternatively, blend in a food processor).

To serve, ladle the soup into bowls, add the reserved potatoes and monk's beard and a dollop of fresh herb pesto. Finally, sprinkle a few wild garlic flowers over the top, if you have them.

Nutrition tip

This soup has lots of heart-healthy ingredients, including potassium, folic acid and sulphur compounds provided by the garlic.

TRY WITH baby courgettes, leeks and peas instead.
ADD a handful of cooked beans or pasta for a minestrone-like soup.
SHREDDED cooked chicken or lamb would make a more substantial soupy-stew.

BLACK BEAN SOUP

I love the sinister jet-black colour of this soup and it makes a great foil to any brightly coloured toppings. I've used avocado, hemp seeds and candy beetroot, but a dollop of soured cream, the sliced green part of a spring onion, diced orange pepper or yellow sweetcorn would all stand out brilliantly against the darkness of the soup.

SERVES 3-4

200g (7oz) dried black beans ❄ 1 bay leaf

1 small onion, cut in half ❄ 2 garlic cloves, peeled and left whole

1 small dried red chilli

600ml (20fl oz) hot Cooked Vegetable Stock (see page 15)

salt and pepper

Put the beans in a bowl, cover with plenty of cold water and leave to soak overnight, then drain.

Place the beans in a large saucepan with the bay leaf, onion, garlic and chilli and cover with fresh cold water. Bring to the boil, then turn the heat down and simmer, part-covered, for about 1 hour, or until tender. When cooked, drain the beans, discard the bay leaf, onion, garlic and chilli and set aside.

To make the soup, return the beans to the pan, pour in the stock and part-blend the beans using a stick blender – keeping some of them whole for a chunky texture. Season to taste with salt and pepper.

To serve, ladle the soup into bowls and add the fixin's of your choice.

Nutrition tip

Black beans are super beans – packed with protein and cell-protective antioxidants (it's the antioxidant components that make them so dark in colour).

SPEED UP the preparation time by using canned black beans.

ADD some crumbled crispy bacon or barbecued pulled pork for a more substantial meal.

A SPRINKLING of grated Cheddar cheese ups the protein content.

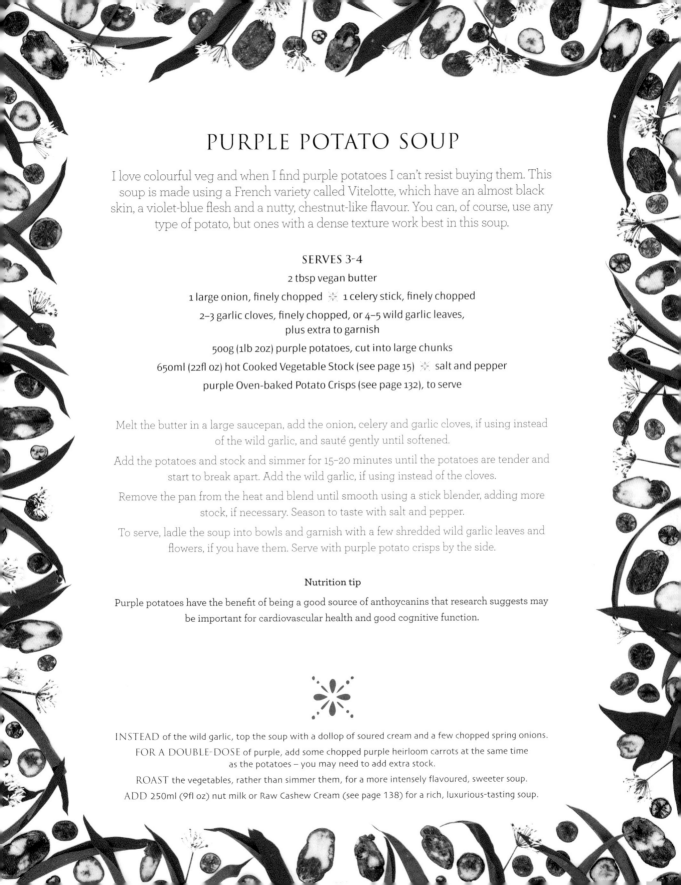

PURPLE POTATO SOUP

I love colourful veg and when I find purple potatoes I can't resist buying them. This soup is made using a French variety called Vitelotte, which have an almost black skin, a violet-blue flesh and a nutty, chestnut-like flavour. You can, of course, use any type of potato, but ones with a dense texture work best in this soup.

SERVES 3-4

2 tbsp vegan butter

1 large onion, finely chopped ❋ 1 celery stick, finely chopped

2–3 garlic cloves, finely chopped, or 4–5 wild garlic leaves, plus extra to garnish

500g (1lb 2oz) purple potatoes, cut into large chunks

650ml (22fl oz) hot Cooked Vegetable Stock (see page 15) ❋ salt and pepper

purple Oven-baked Potato Crisps (see page 132), to serve

Melt the butter in a large saucepan, add the onion, celery and garlic cloves, if using instead of the wild garlic, and sauté gently until softened.

Add the potatoes and stock and simmer for 15–20 minutes until the potatoes are tender and start to break apart. Add the wild garlic, if using instead of the cloves.

Remove the pan from the heat and blend until smooth using a stick blender, adding more stock, if necessary. Season to taste with salt and pepper.

To serve, ladle the soup into bowls and garnish with a few shredded wild garlic leaves and flowers, if you have them. Serve with purple potato crisps by the side.

Nutrition tip

Purple potatoes have the benefit of being a good source of anthoycanins that research suggests may be important for cardiovascular health and good cognitive function.

❋

INSTEAD of the wild garlic, top the soup with a dollop of soured cream and a few chopped spring onions.

FOR A DOUBLE-DOSE of purple, add some chopped purple heirloom carrots at the same time as the potatoes – you may need to add extra stock.

ROAST the vegetables, rather than simmer them, for a more intensely flavoured, sweeter soup.

ADD 250ml (9fl oz) nut milk or Raw Cashew Cream (see page 138) for a rich, luxurious-tasting soup.

CELERY SOUP

Even those who dislike celery usually love this soup!
The flavour of the celery mellows with cooking and is softened by the addition
of soured cream and spiked with a hit of spice from the pink peppercorns.
Celery is naturally salty, so you won't need much seasoning.

SERVES 2-3

1 tbsp olive oil ❄ 1 large onion, finely chopped

2–3 garlic cloves, finely chopped

1 head of celery, sticks separated and thinly sliced and leaves reserved

600ml (20fl oz) hot Cooked Vegetable Stock (see page 15)

1–2 teaspoons pink peppercorns, crushed

100ml (3½fl oz) Raw Soured Cashew Cream (see page 138) or crème fraîche, plus extra to serve

salt and pepper

Heat the oil in a large saucepan, add the onion and garlic and fry gently for a
few minutes until softened but not coloured.

Add the celery and stock and simmer for 15–20 minutes, or until the celery is
soft and cooked through.

Pour the soup into the bowl of a food processor and blitz to a blended but still slightly
chunky texture, or use a stick blender to purée to a smooth consistency.

Stir the pink peppercorns into the soup with the soured cream.
Season to taste with salt and pepper.

To serve, ladle the soup into bowls before topping with the reserved celery leaves
and a drizzle of soured cream.

Nutrition tip

This potassium-rich soup is also a good source of iron if you top it with the cashew cream option.

A BLUE-VEINED CHEESE, such as Stilton or Roquefort, is great crumbled into this soup.
STIR shredded cooked chicken or fresh crabmeat into the soup.
GRATED apple adds a slight sweetness and marries well with the flavour of the celery.

FARRO & PINK RADICCHIO SOUP

Pink radicchio, typically grown in Verona in Italy, is sweeter and less bitter than traditional radicchio, and is great to serve raw in a salad or soup. I've teamed it with farro, a chewy, nutty-tasting grain that works well with the slightly bitter radicchio. Just add extra stock if you prefer a more broth-like consistency.

SERVES 3-4

2 tbsp olive oil ❖ 1 small carrot, finely chopped

1 onion, finely chopped ❖ 200g (7oz) farro

500ml (18fl oz) hot Cooked Vegetable Stock (see page 15)

2 pink radicchio, tough stems removed, leaves separated and large ones cut in half

juice and finely grated zest of 1 orange ❖ salt and pepper

Heat the oil in a large saucepan, add the carrot and onion and cook gently for a few minutes until softened but not coloured.

Stir in the farro then cook briefly for 2–3 minutes before adding the stock. Bring to the boil, then turn the heat down and simmer for 15 minutes. Add the radicchio and cook for a further 5–10 minutes until it has wilted and the farro is tender.

Stir in the orange juice and most of the zest, reserving a little to garnish, and season to taste with salt and pepper.

To serve, ladle the soup into bowls with the reserved orange zest sprinkled over the top.

Nutrition tip

Farro is slightly lower in gluten than many grains and people with mild gluten intolerances can often find it easier to digest.

BROWN OR WILD RICE OR PEARL BARLEY would be good substitutes, if you can't get hold of farro.

TURN the soup into a pink radicchio salad instead: simply mix the radicchio leaves with the cooked farro, onion and carrot and serve it with an orange juice and sumac dressing.

SUNSHINE SOUP

The cheery sunshine yellow colour of this soup comes from the yellow peppers and courgettes, and I've blended it in a food processor to keep it slightly chunky. It's a great soup to make in the summer when courgettes and peppers are plentiful.

SERVES 3-4

1 tablespoon olive oil or coconut oil ❋ 1 onion, finely chopped

1 small carrot, finely chopped ❋ 2 celery sticks, finely chopped

4–5 yellow courgettes, cut into large chunks

2 yellow peppers, deseeded and finely chopped

750ml (1⅓ pints) hot Cooked Vegetable Stock (see page 15)

1 small handful of parsley leaves, roughly chopped

salt and pepper

TO SERVE

1 green courgette ❋ 1 yellow courgette

Heat the oil in a large saucepan, add the onion, carrot and celery and fry gently for a few minutes until softened but not coloured.

Add the courgettes, peppers and stock, season with salt and pepper and simmer gently for 10–15 minutes, or until the courgettes are tender.

Pour the soup into the bowl of a food processor and blend briefly, keeping it slightly chunky.

Before serving, prepare the courgette garnish: score the skin of the green and yellow courgettes lengthways to make shallow, v-shaped grooves then slice very thinly crossways.

To serve, ladle the soup into bowls and top with parsley and the courgette 'flowers'.

Nutrition tip

Yellow peppers contain good amounts of lutein and zeaxanthin, which are antioxidants that can help protect the back of the eye from UV damage.

FOR EXTRA SUBSTANCE, add a few handfuls of cooked grains, such as brown rice, farro or bulgar wheat, or add some cooked pasta.

A DOLLOP of red or green pesto boosts the Mediterranean flavour of the soup.

COCONUT CAULIFLOWER SOUP

This is a great recipe for cauliflower lovers as it gives a double hit of the vegetable! I think it could win over any non-cauli lovers as well, as the smooth and creamy soup is enhanced with coconut milk and fragrant lime leaves. What's more the crispy, pan-fried cauliflower steaks are nothing like cauli as we know it!

SERVES 3-4

1 large cauliflower, outer leaves and tough core removed and cut into large chunks

1–2 tbsp coconut oil ❄ 1 garlic clove, finely chopped

3–4 kaffir lime leaves, finely chopped ❄ 350–400ml (12–14fl oz) coconut milk

300ml (10fl oz) hot Quick No-Recipe Light Vegetable Stock (see page 16)

juice and finely grated zest of 1 lime

salt and pepper ❄ Cauliflower Steaks, to serve (see page 134)

Place the cauliflower in the bowl of a food processor and blitz into very small grains without letting it turn mushy.

Heat the coconut oil in a large saucepan, add the cauliflower and stir-fry for 1–2 minutes over a high heat without colouring.

Turn the heat down, add the garlic and lime leaves, then pour in the coconut milk and stock and simmer gently until the cauliflower is cooked through and forms a soft, pulpy soup. If you prefer a thinner consistency, add a little extra coconut milk, water or stock.

Stir in the lime juice and zest and season to taste with salt and pepper.

To serve, ladle the soup into bowls and top each serving with a cauliflower steak.

Nutrition tip

Cruciferous veg like cauliflower are on a list of 'foods that fight cancer' produced by the American Institute for Cancer Research. Cauliflower is also a good source of pantothenic acid – a B vitamin that helps release energy from the food we eat.

A HANDFUL of chopped coriander adds a herbal freshness.
BLEND the cauli steaks into the soup to give a subtle smoky taste.
USE LESS stock and serve as a side dish to a main meal, such as roast chicken.

WHITE BEAN & RADICCHIO SOUP

This soup is more of a plant-based stew but becomes a beautiful creamy, pale-pink colour when blended. The creaminess and mild flavour of the beans complement and temper the slight bitterness of the radicchio.

SERVES 4-5

400g (14oz) dried haricot beans, rinsed and drained

1 small onion, cut in half ❖ 2 thyme sprigs

2 garlic cloves, peeled ❖ 1 tablespoon olive oil

2 radicchio, tough stems removed, leaves separated and large ones cut in half

800ml (1²/₃ pints) hot Quick No-Recipe Light Vegetable Stock (see page 16)

salt and pepper

TO SERVE

1 small handful of chopped herbs or micro herbs ❖ sprouted seeds or pea shoots

Put the beans in a bowl, cover with plenty of cold water and leave to soak overnight, then drain.

Place the beans in a large saucepan with the onion, thyme and garlic and cover with fresh cold water. Bring to the boil, then turn the heat down and simmer for about 1 hour, or until tender. Drain, discarding the thyme, garlic and onion, and keep the beans warm until ready to use.

Heat the oil in a large sauté pan and add the radicchio. Stir and cook briefly over a medium-high heat until the leaves have wilted. Pour in 100ml (3½fl oz) of the stock, cover with the lid, and simmer gently for 10 minutes, or until the radicchio is cooked through. Add the cooked beans to the pan with the remaining stock.

Remove the pan from the heat and blend until smooth and creamy using a stick blender. Season to taste with salt and pepper.

To serve, ladle the soup into bowls and scatter the herbs and sprouted seeds or pea shoots over the top.

Nutrition tip

Radicchio contains good levels of lutein and vitamin E, while you'll get a good level of magnesium – important for energy production and a healthy nervous system – from the haricot beans.

SHORT OF TIME? Try using canned haricot beans instead.

SERVE topped with grated Parmesan or cheese-flavoured nutritional yeast flakes.

STIR IN some finely shredded raw radicchio just before serving, and add a dollop of pesto for extra colour, texture and flavour.

NON-VEGETARIANS may like to add cooked diced chorizo.

THREE TOMATO SOUP

This simple soup uses three different types of tomatoes as well as garlic and fresh herbs. You could also add some tomato purée to give it another layer of tomatoey flavour!

SERVES 3-4

1 small handful of sun-dried tomatoes, roughly chopped

2 tablespoons olive oil ❄ 2 onions, finely chopped

3–4 garlic cloves, finely chopped ❄ 300g (10½oz) ripe tomatoes

300g (10½oz) canned chopped tomatoes ❄ pinch of sugar

1 large handful of mixed herbs, such as thyme, oregano, marjoram, sage and basil, plus extra to garnish

salt and pepper

Place the sun-dried tomatoes in a bowl and pour over enough boiling water to cover. Add a pinch of salt and leave to stand for 20–30 minutes until softened, then drain.

Heat the oil in a large saucepan, add the onions and garlic and sauté gently until softened.

Add the drained sun-dried and fresh tomatoes and simmer for 10–15 minutes until the fresh tomatoes have softened and rendered their juices. Stir in the canned tomatoes, sugar and herbs. Season to taste with salt and pepper, and simmer for a further 10 minutes.

Remove the pan from the heat and blend the mixture until smooth, using a stick blender or in a food processor, or leave it slightly chunky for a more rustic texture.

To serve, ladle the soup into bowls and serve with a few extra fresh herbs scattered over the top.

Nutrition tip

You'll get a big boost of tomato lycopene from this soup – studies suggest this could help reduce your risk of heart disease and potentially protect your skin against UV damage too.

SPOON the soup over grilled country bread rubbed with garlic or just serve with toasted crusty bread.

SERVE as a sauce over pasta, or as the base of a Bolognese or ragù sauce.

FOR EXTRA SUBSTANCE, stir in a handful of long-grain rice, add about 200ml (7fl oz) water and simmer until the rice is cooked.

SWEETCORN SOUP

This golden yellow soup is very creamy, and without the addition of any dairy products. The acidity of the balsamic vinegar cuts through the natural sweetness of the corn helping to balance out the flavours. Serve warm or chilled.

SERVES 2-3

4 corn-on-the-cobs, outer husks removed ✻ 1 tablespoon olive oil
1 onion, finely chopped ✻ 2 garlic cloves, finely chopped
2 celery sticks, finely chopped ✻ 1 white potato, peeled and finely chopped
1 teaspoon thyme leaves ✻ 450ml (16fl oz) hot Cooked Vegetable Stock (see page 15)
1 tablespoon balsamic vinegar ✻ salt and pepper

Stand a corn-on-the-cob upright on a board and slice off the kernels. Repeat with the remaining corn cobs.

Toast the kernels from one of the cobs in a large, dry, nonstick frying pan for 4–5 minutes until golden and crisp. Set aside until ready to serve the soup.

Heat the oil in a large saucepan or sauté pan, add the onion, garlic and celery and fry gently until softened.

Add the potato, remaining raw sweetcorn kernels, thyme and stock. Bring to the boil then let it bubble away gently for 20–30 minutes, covered, or until the potato is cooked through.

Remove the pan from the heat and blend the soup until smooth and creamy using a stick blender, or tip it into a food processor and process lightly for a slightly chunkier texture. Season to taste with salt and pepper.

To serve, ladle the soup into bowls, scatter over the toasted corn and drizzle with the balsamic vinegar.

Nutrition tip

Yellow corn is a good source of lutein and zeaxanthin, antioxidants that are associated, in particular, with good eye health.

✻

ADD cooked seafood, such as prawns, crab, squid, clams or smoked haddock, to create the flavours of a traditional chowder.

FROZEN OR CANNED sweetcorn can be used instead of fresh.

SWEET POTATO SOUP

This makes a beautiful deep-golden soup; I like to offset its colour with a contrasting purple topping. I've used finely shredded radicchio and purple-tinged mint leaves in the photograph, but purple basil or chopped red chard stems, purple shiso leaves or sprouting beetroot seeds all look beautiful, too.

I've also added a topping of grated raw sweet potato as it's surprisingly good eaten raw and gives a contrast in texture to the velvety smooth soup. The spiced crispy chickpeas are a great alternative to crunchy bread croutons.

SERVES 4

2 tablespoons olive oil or coconut oil ❊ 1 large white or red onion, finely chopped

2–3 garlic cloves, finely chopped ❊ 1 teaspoon ras-el-hanout spice mix, plus extra for sprinkling

3 large sweet potatoes, peeled and coarsely grated

1.2 litres (2 pints) hot Cooked Vegetable Stock (see page 15) ❊ 2 tablespoons tahini

salt and pepper

TO SERVE

Spiced Roasted Chickpeas (see page 134)

1 handful of purple mint leaves ❊ few radicchio leaves, shredded

Heat the oil in a large saucepan, add the onion and garlic and fry gently until softened, then add the ras-el-hanout and cook, stirring, for a further few minutes, or until the spices release their fragrance.

Add the sweet potatoes, reserving a little to garnish, and stock. Bring to the boil, then turn the heat down and simmer for 10–15 minutes, or until the sweet potatoes are tender and cooked through. Stir in the tahini.

Remove the pan from the heat and blend until silky smooth using a stick blender or in a food processor.

To serve, ladle the soup into bowls and top with the roasted chickpeas, the reserved grated sweet potato, an extra sprinkling of ras-el-hanout, herbs and radicchio.

Nutrition tip

Full of slow-release energy, sweet potatoes are higher in vitamins C and E than normal potatoes, plus the yellow colour denotes beta-carotene, which the body can use to make vitamin A.

STIR IN some cooked shredded chicken or pulled pork to turn this into a more substantial meal.
ADD cooked mini minted lamb meatballs and a handful of cooked couscous for a Moroccan-type stew.

RED LENTIL SOUP

This is a simple, comforting soup that you can cook quite quickly as the lentils don't need pre-soaking. If you don't like it too spicy, reduce the amount of dried and fresh chilli, or leave out altogether. I've served the soup with roasted caramelized carrots and crushed toasted cashew nuts, but you could try it with a raw grated carrot salad.

SERVES 2-3

3–4 large carrots, preferably purple ones, cut into large chunks or batons

2 tablespoons olive oil or melted coconut oil ✳ 1–2 teaspoons maple syrup

1 onion, finely chopped ✳ 1 small red chilli, deseeded and finely chopped

2.5cm (1in) piece fresh root ginger, peeled and grated ✳ 2 garlic cloves, finely chopped

½ teaspoon dried red chilli flakes, plus extra for sprinkling

¼ teaspoon ground cumin or coriander ✳ 200g (7oz) split red lentils, rinsed and drained

600ml (20fl oz) hot Cooked Vegetable Stock (see page 15) ✳ 2 tablespoons cashew nuts

salt and pepper

Preheat the oven to 200°C (400°F) Gas Mark 6.

To caramelize the carrots, put them in a bowl and mix with 1 tablespoon of the oil, the maple syrup and some seasoning. Tip them into a roasting tray and roast in the oven for 20–30 minutes, or until tender and golden.

While the carrots are roasting make the soup: heat the remaining oil in a large saucepan, add the onion, fresh red chilli, ginger and garlic and fry gently for 4–5 minutes until softened. Add the chilli flakes and cumin or coriander and cook, stirring, for a few minutes.

Add the red lentils and stock. Bring to the boil, then turn the heat down and simmer, part-covered, for 20 minutes, or until the lentils are tender.

Before serving, toast the cashew nuts. Put the cashews in a large, dry frying pan and toast over a medium heat for 3–4 minutes, tossing the pan occasionally, until golden all over. Tip the nuts into a bowl and leave to cool, then finely chop.

To serve, ladle the soup into bowls, top with the roasted carrots, toasted cashews and a sprinkling of chilli flakes.

Nutrition tip

Red lentils are a good plant source of iron, and serving with the toasted cashews adds a second burst of this anaemia-protective mineral too.

A DOLLOP of natural yogurt and a handful of chopped coriander leaves would also make a great topping.

SERVE with grilled flatbread or naan bread.

ADD some cubes of oven-roasted tofu or grilled aubergine.

USE less stock and serve as a lentil dahl or accompaniment.

BLACK-EYED BEAN CHILLI SOUP

This recipe is a combination of chilli-flavoured greens and creamy-textured black-eyed beans. You can blend everything to make a thick, creamy soup, or stir the whole beans into the blended greens. I've served the soup with a swirl of green herb oil and a cooling dollop of vegan soured cream to temper the heat slightly.

SERVES 3-4

200g (7oz) dried black-eyed beans, rinsed and drained

2 tablespoons olive oil or coconut oil ❋ 1 large onion, finely chopped

2–3 garlic cloves, finely chopped ❋ 2 fresh green chillies, deseeded and finely chopped

4–5 cavolo nero leaves, tough stalks removed and leaves torn into 2.5cm (1in) pieces

pinch of dried chilli powder ❋ 2 large handfuls of baby spinach leaves

3–4 spring onions, finely chopped ❋ 250ml (9fl oz) hot Cooked Vegetable Stock (see page 15)

1 Baby Gem lettuce, finely shredded ❋ salt and pepper

TO SERVE

Raw Soured Cashew Cream (see page 138) ❋ Green Herb Oil (see page 135)

Put the beans in a bowl, cover with plenty of cold water and leave to soak overnight, then drain.

Place the beans in a large saucepan, cover with fresh cold water and bring to the boil, then turn the heat down and simmer, part-covered, for about 1 hour, or until tender. Drain the beans and set aside until ready to use.

Heat the oil in a large sauté pan. Fry the onion, garlic and green chillies gently until softened.

Stir in the cavolo nero and chilli powder, cover and cook for 5–6 minutes until the leaves have wilted. Stir in the spinach and spring onions and cook for another few minutes, stirring occasionally, until the spinach has wilted.

Add the stock and lettuce. Blend using a stick blender, leaving the greens partly blended if you prefer. Stir in the cooked beans and reheat briefly, if needed, then season to taste.

To serve, ladle the soup into bowls and top with a dollop of raw soured cream and a drizzle of herb oil.

Nutrition tip

All the lovely deep greens in this soup make it a good source of iron, vitamin C and vitamin A.

❋

TRY SERVING with warm corn tortillas and topped with diced avocado.

USE canned black-eyed beans for a quick alternative to dried beans.

SHREDDED ham hock, slow-cooked pork or crumbled crispy bacon or pancetta also work well in this soup.

SPRING NOODLE SOUP

This simple noodle soup is fragrant and filling without being heavy. It uses translucent, gluten-free rice noodles, which are simmered in a flavoursome broth. Any tender young green vegetables work well as the green element in this soup.

SERVES 2-3

1 teaspoon sesame oil ✳ 2–3 garlic cloves, finely chopped

1 small green chilli, deseeded and chopped ✳ 3 spring onions, finely chopped

2.5cm (1in) piece fresh root ginger, peeled and finely chopped

4–5 asparagus spears, woody ends broken off, chopped into 2.5cm (1in) lengths

70g (2½oz) fresh or frozen peas ✳ 1 small handful of agretti (monk's beard) or samphire

600ml (20fl oz) hot Cooked Vegetable Stock (see page 15)

3 bundles of rice noodles, about 225g (8oz) total weight

juice and finely grated zest of 1 lime ✳ 1 tablespoon hoisin sauce ✳ salt and pepper

TO SERVE

1 teaspoon black sesame seeds

1 small handful of pea shoots or fragrant herbs, such as coriander

Heat the sesame oil in a large saucepan or sauté pan, add the garlic, chilli, spring onions and ginger and fry gently until softened.

Add the asparagus, peas, agretti and stock and simmer, covered, for 5–10 minutes until the vegetables are tender.

Add the rice noodles, stir and simmer for a further 3 minutes or until the noodles are cooked and tender. Stir in the lime juice and zest and hoisin sauce. Season to taste with salt and pepper.

To serve, ladle the soup into bowls and top with the black sesame seeds and pea shoots or herbs.

Nutrition tip

Soluble and prebiotic fibres in the peas and asparagus make this light soup a good one for the health of your digestive tract and cardiovascular system.

ADD stir-fried marinated mushrooms, tofu or shredded cooked chicken.
CRUSHED dry-roasted or toasted peanuts would also make a good crunchy topping.

ALPHABET SOUP

You can make this soup using dried alphabet pasta but making your own letter shapes is a much healthier option and a great way to encourage kids to get more of the good stuff down! You can add the letters to any soup or salad, or steam them and serve as a side dish. They are best cut from firm raw vegetables, such as sweet potato, carrots, beetroot, mooli or jicama.

SERVES 2-3
1 large sweet potato, peeled and thinly sliced into rounds
1 large carrot, thinly sliced into rounds
1 large raw beetroot or candy beetroot, thinly sliced into rounds
680ml (23fl oz) Quick No-Recipe Light Vegetable Stock (see page 16)
1 small handful of chopped mixed herbs, such as parsley, basil, dill and chives
salt and pepper

Using cookie cutters, cut out alphabet letters from the sweet potato, carrot and beetroot – save any leftover scraps to use in a stew, salad or juice.

Gently heat the vegetable broth and stir in the letters and herbs, reserving a few to garnish. Simmer for a few minutes to warm everything through then check the seasoning.

To serve, ladle the broth into bowls and scatter over a few extra herbs.

Nutrition tip
This soup provides vitamin A, and the nitrate-rich beetroot helps opens up blood vessels and reduce blood pressure.

STIR in a handful of finely sliced leafy greens, such as baby kale, spinach or swiss chard, fresh peas, grated carrot, cooked haricot beans or small pasta shapes for a more substantial meal or in place of the alphabet letters.

SHREDDED cooked meat such as chicken or flaked cooked fish would work well too.

WHITE SPROUTING BROCCOLI SOUP

White sprouting broccoli is such a seasonal treat and is far less cabbagey in flavour than the purple sprouting variety. If you can't get hold of either, regular broccoli can be used instead. I've used vegan butter to give a more luxurious, creamy taste, but substitute with olive oil, coconut oil or regular butter, if you prefer.

SERVES 3-4

2 tablespoons vegan butter ❋ 1 small onion, finely chopped

2 courgettes, roughly chopped ❋ 2 large bunches of white sprouting broccoli, roughly chopped

600ml (20fl oz) hot Quick No-Recipe Light Vegetable Stock (see page 16)

juice and finely grated zest of 1 lemon ❋ salt and pepper

Heat the butter in a large saucepan, add the onion and fry gently for a few minutes until softened but not coloured.

Add the courgettes and broccoli, cover and sauté for 5–10 minutes until the broccoli starts to wilt.

Pour in the vegetable stock, cover and simmer for 15–20 minutes until the courgettes and broccoli are cooked – keep them slightly al dente, if you prefer.

Remove the pan from the heat and purée or part-blend the soup, using a stick blender or in a food processor. Season to taste with salt and pepper.

To serve, ladle the soup into bowls and stir in the lemon juice and zest just before serving.

Nutrition tip

White sprouting broccoli has all the benefits of normal broccoli, so this soup is a good source of folic acid and beta-carotene.

TRY using the zest and juice of 1 orange instead of the lemon.
SPRINKLE with an orange or lemon-based Gremolata or Pangritata (see pages 130 and 131), before serving.
FOR NON-VEGANS, crumble over crispy smoked streaky bacon or feta cheese.

MATZO BALL SOUP

A vegan version of the classic chicken broth with dumplings. The egg in the traditional dumplings is substituted for flaxseeds, which act as a binding agent when combined with water. A scattering of fried sage leaves gives a delicate savoury crunch.

SERVES 2-3

FOR THE VEGETABLE BROTH

1 tbsp olive oil ❖ 2 garlic cloves, finely chopped ❖ 1 onion, finely chopped

2 spring onions, finely chopped ❖ 2 large carrots, finely chopped ❖ 3–4 mushrooms, finely chopped

3 celery sticks, finely chopped ❖ 600ml (20fl oz) hot Cooked Vegetable Stock (see page 15)

1 small handful of flat-leaf parsley, leaves finely chopped

salt and pepper ❖ Crispy Sage Leaves (see page 132), to garnish

FOR THE MATZO BALLS

150g (5½oz) matzo meal, or dry crackers crushed into fine breadcrumbs

2 tbsp ground flaxseeds ❖ 1 tbsp whole flaxseeds ❖ 3 tbsp quinoa flakes

1 tbsp chopped fresh dill ❖ ½ tsp onion salt ❖ 100ml (3½fl oz) water

First make the matzo balls: mix together everything except the water in a large mixing bowl, then stir in the measured water and season to taste. Leave to stand for 5–10 minutes to thicken. Stir in extra water, if needed, at this point – you want to achieve a slightly moist but 'mouldable' consistency.

To shape the matzo balls, spoon or pinch heaped teaspoons of the mixture and roll between your hands into balls. Bring a large pan of salted water to the boil, place the matzo balls in the water and cook at a robust simmer for 30–40 minutes until cooked right through. When cooked, place on a kitchen paper-lined plate and set aside until required.

While the balls are cooking, make the broth. Heat the oil in a large saucepan or sauté pan, add the garlic, onion, spring onions, carrots, mushrooms and celery and fry gently until softened. Add the stock and simmer for 10–15 minutes until the vegetables are just tender. Stir in the parsley and season to taste.

Drop the matzo balls into the broth. Simmer briefly to bring both up to eating temperature.

To serve, ladle the broth into bowls before scattering over a handful of crispy sage leaves.

Nutrition tip

The quinoa and flax in the matzo balls bump up levels of protein, omega-3 and the mineral magnesium.

FINELY SHREDDED CABBAGE, Swiss chard and leeks work well in the broth and increase the vegetable content. GROUND ALMONDS work well in place of quinoa flakes.

ROOT SOUP

This speedy root vegetable soup is made with the same three primary ingredients as the rostis that they are served with. Both recipes start off in the same grated format, so it's easy to make both at the same time.

SERVES 4-6

2 raw beetroots, coarsely grated ❊ 2 large carrots, coarsely grated

2 large parsnips, coarsely grated ❊ 2 garlic cloves, finely chopped

800ml (1⅓ pints) hot Cooked Vegetable Stock (see page 15)

salt and pepper ❊ Root Vegetable Rosti (see page 132), to serve

Simply place all the ingredients, except the rosti, in a large saucepan and bring to a simmer. Cook for 10–15 minutes until the veg is tender.

Remove the pan from the heat and blend until completely smooth, using a stick blender or in a food processor. Season to taste with salt and pepper.

To serve, ladle the soup into bowls and top each serving with a rosti.

Nutrition tip

This is comfort food without the calories – and a great source of potassium and natural nitrates that will help to keep your blood pressure healthy.

A FEW TABLESPOONS of Raw Cashew Cream (see page 138) or crème fraîche will add a rich creaminess.

COMPLEMENT the flavours of the soup and rosti with a scattering of flaked smoked fish, such as salmon or mackerel. A squeeze of lemon and a sprinkling of fresh dill would taste good, too.

SPEEDY PEA SOUP

This is a super simple, speedy soup that can be ready in 15 minutes. You can blend it completely so it's smooth or leave some peas whole for a bit of texture. Cooking the garlic first gives it a head start on the peas and tempers its strong flavour. Crisp and crunchy toppings are the perfect contrast to the silky, smooth soup.

SERVES 3-4

4–5 garlic cloves, peeled and left whole ✳ 300g (10½oz) frozen peas
450ml (16fl oz) hot Cooked Vegetable Stock (see page 15)
2–3 tbsp Raw Cashew Cream (see page 138) or crème fraîche
1 small handful of mint leaves ✳ salt and pepper

TO SERVE

Crispy Sprout Leaves (see page 132) ✳ Savoury Granola (see page 131)

Put the garlic cloves in a large saucepan and just cover with cold water. Bring the water to the boil and simmer for 5 minutes until tender.

Add the peas and stock and simmer for a further 5–7 minutes until the peas are just cooked through. Add the cashew cream and mint leaves.

Remove the pan from the heat and blend until silky smooth, using a stick blender or in a food processor. Season to taste with salt and pepper.

To serve, ladle the soup into bowls and top with the crispy sprout leaves and savoury granola.

Nutrition tip

Frozen peas contain good amounts of iron and thiamin (a B vitamin that helps to release energy from food) as well as soluble fibre.

ADD diced smoked cooked ham, pancetta or shredded salami or prosciutto.
USE fresh tarragon, coriander or dill as alternatives to the mint.
SERVE as mushy peas, a dip or as a topping for crostini, reducing the quantity of stock to give the soup a thicker consistency.

ROASTED AUBERGINE SOUP

This pale-coloured, velvety smooth soup gets its lovely smoky flavour and creamy taste from the roasted and blended aubergines, and can be eaten warm or chilled. Pangritata (see page 131) adds a complementary citrus taste and savoury crunch.

SERVES 2

2 aubergines, cut into 2.5cm (1in) dice ✳ 4 tbsp olive oil

1 onion, finely chopped ✳ 3–4 garlic cloves, peeled

400ml (14fl oz) hot Cooked Vegetable Stock (see page 15)

juice of 1 lemon, plus extra to serve ✳ salt and pepper

Pangritata (see page 131), to serve

Preheat the oven to 220°C (425°F) Gas Mark 7, and heat two roasting trays.

Place the aubergines in a bowl and toss with 3 tablespoons of the oil until lightly coated. Tip the aubergines onto the heated roasting trays and spread out in a single, even layer. Roast for 20–30 minutes until light golden on all sides.

While the aubergines are roasting, heat the remaining oil in a large, deep saucepan, add the onion and garlic and cook over a medium heat until softened but not coloured.

When the aubergine is cooked, add it to the pan with the stock, lemon juice and salt and pepper.

Remove the pan from the heat and purée until silky smooth using a stick blender. Add more stock, if you prefer a thinner consistency, and additional lemon juice and seasoning to taste.

To serve, ladle the soup into bowls and serve with the pangritata sprinkled over and an extra squeeze of lemon juice, if desired – or you could add a drizzle of lemon oil.

Nutrition tip

Nasunin, an anthocyanin found in aubergines, has been shown in laboratory studies to protect the delicate fats in brain cell membranes.

✳

CRUMBLE over feta cheese or crispy fried anchovies for an extra flavour boost.

A SPRINKLE of Za'atar (see page 128) or a pinch of smoked paprika is lovely with this soup.

SERVE as a dip by reducing the quantity of water slightly – it's almost like a baba ganoush.

FOR AN EXTRA SMOKY FLAVOUR, instead of roasting the aubergines in the oven, char the aubergines under the grill or on a barbecue then remove their blackened skin before puréeing the flesh.

SAVOURY OAT SOUP

Not just for breakfast! Rolled oats are a great gluten-free option for thickening soups and stews and can be left whole for a chunky texture or blended in to give a rich, creamy consistency. You can stir the oats into a warm soup and eat straightaway, or cook them for longer so they thicken further, or just stir them into a savoury broth and leave to soak in the fridge overnight for a savoury porridge to eat in the morning. Here, I've mixed the oats with a quick tomato soup. A green cashew drizzle lifts the flavour and adds a shot of colour and chlorophyll.

SERVES 2-3

½ tbsp olive oil ✳ 1–2 garlic cloves, finely chopped

350g (12oz) cherry tomatoes, cut in half ✳ 1 small handful of basil leaves

½ tsp coconut sugar or sweetener of choice

100g (3½oz) rolled porridge oats ✳ salt and pepper

Green Cashew Drizzle (see page 137), to serve

Heat the oil in a wide saucepan or sauté pan, add the garlic and cook gently without browning.

Add the tomatoes, basil and sugar and cook, covered, for 10–15 minutes, stirring occasionally, or until the tomatoes have rendered their liquid and softened to a pulpy consistency. Season to taste with salt and pepper.

Stir in the oats and add a little water to thin, if needed. Simmer for a further few minutes until the oats are warmed through, or cook for longer until the oats are softened and make a thicker, creamier soup.

To serve, ladle the soup into bowls and top with the green cashew drizzle.

Nutrition tip

Oats contain the soluble fibre beta glucan, which has been shown to help keep blood cholesterol levels in check.

✳

A GREAT 'TRAVELLING' SOUP – just place the uncooked oats in a flask with the warm tomato mixture and let them cook slowly in the liquid until you're ready to eat the soup.

FINELY DICED chorizo or spicy cured meat stirred into this soup will entice non-vegans.

TRY CRUMBLING over goats' cheese or crispy bacon, or serve with a poached or softly boiled egg.

BLUE SPIRULINA SOUP

You'll have noticed by now that I love vibrant, colourful soups so to complete the spectrum, here's a soup that's blue! This is a savoury soup that's made with healthy raw veg and spirulina powder (which is what makes it blue) and is like a savoury smoothie, just eaten from a bowl.

SERVES 2-3

½ head of cauliflower, broken into small florets

1 avocado, cut in half, stone removed and flesh scooped out

1 shallot, roughly chopped ❄ 50g (1¾oz) cashew nuts

½ small garlic clove ❄ 200ml (7fl oz) coconut water

1 tsp spirulina powder ❄ salt and pepper

1 apple, chopped into matchsticks, to serve

Grate or crumble a few of the cauliflower florets into a rice-like texture and reserve to garnish the top of the soup.

Put the remaining cauliflower into a high-speed blender with the rest of the ingredients, apart from the apple, and blend until smooth and creamy.

To serve, pour the soup into bowls and top with the apple and grated cauliflower.

Nutrition tip

Spirulina is a superfood algae and a rich source of plant-based protein, omega-3, vitamins B1, B2, B3, copper, iron, antioxidants and a whole host of other valuable nutrients, too. With so many nutrient-packed ingredients in this soup, it's the perfect all round health tonic.

SERVE CHILLED, just place in the fridge for 2–3 hours or until ready to eat.

YOU COULD USE green spirulina, blue-green algae powder, chlorella powder or wheatgrass powder as an alternative to the blue spirulina.

DRESS courgetti or sweet potato noodles with the soup, for a quirky-looking main dish.

RAW PEPPER, ORANGE & TOMATO SOUP

This vibrant, raw, savoury soup has a combination of sweet, sour and spicy flavours. Serve it simply or, as I've shown here, with the addition of orange slices, sourdough croutons (see below), preserved mini peppers and a drizzle of Raw Soured Cashew Cream (see page 138).

SERVES 2-3

3 large red or orange peppers, deseeded and roughly chopped

1 small red chilli, deseeded and roughly chopped

400g (14oz) ripe tomatoes, cut into large chunks

3 large blood oranges, peeled ❉ 300ml (10fl oz) carrot juice

salt and pepper

Place all the ingredients in a food processor or high-speed blender and blitz until thick and smooth.

To serve, ladle the soup into bowls and serve with your choice of toppings.

Nutrition tip

Brimming with vitamins A and C, this soup makes a really big contribution to topping up your immune defences. It will help keep your skin vibrant and heathy, too.

TO MAKE THE CROUTONS, fry torn up pieces of sourdough bread in olive oil or butter until crisp and golden,

FOR AN EXTRA-SAVOURY FLAVOUR, add a small garlic clove before blending. Grate over a little orange zest before serving for extra zing.

STRAWBERRY SOUP

Chilled strawberry soup is a lovely way to end a meal and it also makes the most of a summertime glut of strawberries. A swirl of sweetened cashew cream gives this sweet soup a luxurious feel and an added creamy texture.

SERVES 2-3

250g (9oz) ripe strawberries ❋ 100ml (3½fl oz) coconut water
150ml (5fl oz) coconut yogurt ❋ Vanilla Cashew Cream (see page 138), to serve

Wash the strawberries well, cut off the green tops (if you're using organic strawberries reserve the tops to use in a smoothie or juice) and roughly chop the fruit.

Place the strawberries in a high-speed blender with the coconut water and yogurt and blend until smooth. Cover and chill in the fridge for 2–3 hours, or until ready to serve.

To serve, ladle the soup into bowls or chilled glasses and add a swirl of cashew cream on top.

Nutrition tip

Strawberries provide more vitamin C than oranges, and they're also packed with heart-friendly anthocyanin antioxidants and folic acid.

FREEZE in ice lolly moulds or a freezer-proof container for a healthy ice cream.
ADD a few ice cubes to the soup, or a swirl of balsamic vinegar to enhance the flavour of the strawberries.
A GOOD VEGAN ALTERNATIVE to traditional yogurt is coconut yogurt, but if you eat dairy products try Greek yogurt or any thick, mild, natural yogurt.

SPARKLING PINEAPPLE SOUP

This can be served as an inter-course palate cleanser, as you would a sorbet, or as a sweet, refreshing end to a meal. Serve in chilled glass cups, cocktail glasses, or, if you keep the mixture thick, in delicate glass bowls with a spoon. The saffron powder enhances the golden colour of the fruity soup, but don't add too much of it.

SERVES 3-4

½ pineapple, peeled, cored and chopped into chunks
2.5cm (1in) piece fresh root ginger, peeled and chopped
splash of coconut water (optional)
300ml (10fl oz) Prosecco, Champagne or sparkling wine
few pinches of saffron powder, to decorate

Run the pineapple and ginger through a juicer if you want a thin liquid, or blend in a high-speed blender with a splash of coconut water or water to give a thick, smoothie-like consistency.

To serve, pour 2 tablespoons of the pineapple and ginger mix into each glass and top up with Prosecco, Champagne or sparkling wine. Finally, sprinkle over a tiny pinch of saffron and swirl it into the foamy top.

Nutrition tip

Fresh pineapple contains a compound called bromelain, which is thought to act as a natural digestive aid.

FREEZE the pineapple and ginger mixture to make a sorbet, granita or alcoholic ice pops.
FOR A lovely tropical, non-alcoholic drink, substitute coconut water for the Prosecco.
SERVE poured over a fresh fruit salad for a sweet, bubbly dessert.

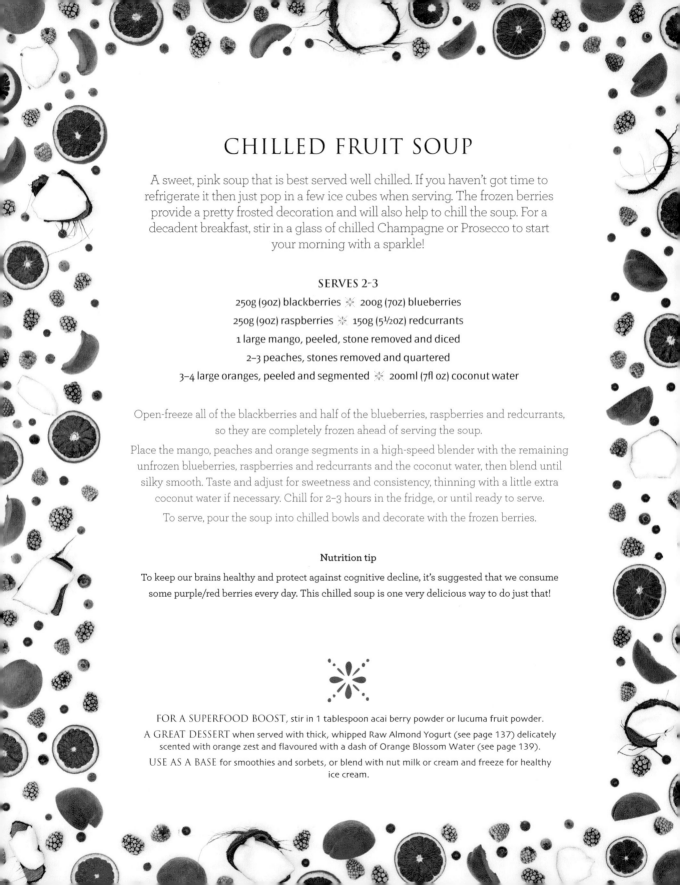

CHILLED FRUIT SOUP

A sweet, pink soup that is best served well chilled. If you haven't got time to refrigerate it then just pop in a few ice cubes when serving. The frozen berries provide a pretty frosted decoration and will also help to chill the soup. For a decadent breakfast, stir in a glass of chilled Champagne or Prosecco to start your morning with a sparkle!

SERVES 2-3

250g (9oz) blackberries ✳ 200g (7oz) blueberries

250g (9oz) raspberries ✳ 150g (5½oz) redcurrants

1 large mango, peeled, stone removed and diced

2–3 peaches, stones removed and quartered

3–4 large oranges, peeled and segmented ✳ 200ml (7fl oz) coconut water

Open-freeze all of the blackberries and half of the blueberries, raspberries and redcurrants, so they are completely frozen ahead of serving the soup.

Place the mango, peaches and orange segments in a high-speed blender with the remaining unfrozen blueberries, raspberries and redcurrants and the coconut water, then blend until silky smooth. Taste and adjust for sweetness and consistency, thinning with a little extra coconut water if necessary. Chill for 2–3 hours in the fridge, or until ready to serve.

To serve, pour the soup into chilled bowls and decorate with the frozen berries.

Nutrition tip

To keep our brains healthy and protect against cognitive decline, it's suggested that we consume some purple/red berries every day. This chilled soup is one very delicious way to do just that!

✳

FOR A SUPERFOOD BOOST, stir in 1 tablespoon acai berry powder or lucuma fruit powder.

A GREAT DESSERT when served with thick, whipped Raw Almond Yogurt (see page 137) delicately scented with orange zest and flavoured with a dash of Orange Blossom Water (see page 139).

USE AS A BASE for smoothies and sorbets, or blend with nut milk or cream and freeze for healthy ice cream.

CHILLED PERSIAN YOGURT SOUP

This is a lovely light soup that can be made sweet or savoury. I've used a homemade sweetened Raw Almond Yogurt (see page 137), but you can substitute it with a shop-bought vegan or dairy yogurt, sweetened or not. I've topped the soup with fragrant herbs, flowers and nuts that can also be stirred into the soup and left to infuse their flavour for 2–3 hours, or overnight in the fridge if more convenient.

SERVES 2-3

450ml (16fl oz) Raw Almond Yogurt (see page 137) or yogurt of choice

1–2 tbsp Orange Blossom Water or Rose Water (see page 139)

1 handful of ice cubes ❋ 1–2 tsp maple syrup or sweetener of your choice (optional)

TO SERVE

1 tbsp pistachio nuts, roughly chopped ❋ ¼ tsp pink peppercorns, crushed

1 tbsp finely chopped fragrant herbs, such as dill, mint or fennel fronds

1 tbsp fresh or dried edible rose petals, or other fragrant edible flowers

Place the yogurt, orange blossom water or rose water, ice and maple syrup, if using, in a high-speed blender and blitz until smooth.

To serve, pour the soup into chilled bowls and serve with the pistachios, peppercorns, herbs and flowers sprinkled over the top.

Nutrition tip

This is a rich source of calcium (particularly if made with dairy yogurt). Using maple syrup keeps the glycaemic index (rate at which it raises blood sugar) healthily low.

FREEZE the soup into lolly moulds for a creamy frozen treat, or use as the base of a smoothie.

GOLDEN RAISINS would be a nice addition to this soup.

FOR A SAVOURY VERSION, use unsweetened yogurt and flavour with herbs, such as sage, thyme, coriander, chives, oregano and rosemary, as well as spices, including Za'atar (see page 128), sumac or garam masala. Cucumber, chilli, pine nuts or walnuts are also good additions to a savoury variety.

CHILLED SWEET YOGURT SOUP

This sweet, vibrant soup is great served chilled as a dessert, and the tartness of the raspberries and yogurt offset the natural sweetness of the strawberries. I've used homemade almond yogurt, but coconut yogurt, or any other dairy or vegan alternative would be suitable.

SERVES 3-4

400g (14oz) raspberries ❄ 150ml (5fl oz) chilled coconut water

200g (7oz) strawberries, hulled and cut in half

200ml (7fl oz) chilled Raw Almond Yogurt (see page 137)

1 small handful of edible flowers, such as violets, borage, fuchsias, marigolds or primroses, to decorate

Place the raspberries and coconut water in a high-speed blender or food processor and blend to a thick purée. Pour out of the blender and set aside.

Place the strawberries in the blender with half of the almond yogurt and blend to make a thick pale pink 'soup'.

To serve, pour the strawberry soup into individual bowls, then add the raspberry purée and the remaining raw almond yogurt and swirl together to make a decorative marbled pattern on the top. Decorate with a few edible flowers, just before serving.

Nutrition tip

Berries like raspberries and strawberries are rich in anthocyanins, thought to offer protection against cardiovascular disease and cognitive decline.

FREEZE the 'soup' in ice pops or in a freezer-proof container to make a healthy ice cream.
You can layer the different colours (freezing after pouring in each layer) to create striped ice cream lollies.

USE as a base for a smoothie.

POUR over a bowl of fresh or frozen berries, such as strawberries, raspberries, blueberries and redcurrants, for a type of sweet fruit 'stew'.

SCATTER over a handful of chopped nuts or flaked coconut, or swirl in a dollop of raspberry chia jam.

CHOCOLATE PUDDLE SOUP

When I was young, my best friend's mother would make us something very similar to this as a treat, except her version was laden with white sugar. This recipe is based on much healthier ingredients, including avocado, frozen bananas and raw chocolate. Thin the mixture with extra coconut water if you want a drinkable sweet soup, otherwise serve in bowls as a spoonable pudding.

SERVES 3-4

2 bananas, peeled, chopped into chunks and frozen

1 large ripe avocado, cut in half, stone removed and flesh scooped out

2–3 tbsp raw cacao powder ❄ 100ml (3½fl oz) coconut water

1 tsp maple syrup, date paste or sweetener of choice (optional)

TO SERVE

sliced strawberries ❄ pomegranate seeds

cacao nibs ❄ freeze-dried raspberry pieces

Put the frozen bananas into a food processor or high-speed blender with the avocado, cacao powder and sweetener, if using, and blend to a smooth, thick consistency. Thin the mixture down with extra coconut water, if too thick, then chill the sweet soup in the fridge until ready to serve.

To serve, pour or spoon the soup into bowls and decorate the top with sliced strawberries, pomegranate seeds, raw cacao nibs and freeze-dried raspberry pieces.

Nutrition tip

With very little added sugar, you can enjoy this chocolate treat guilt-free. It's a good source of potassium and monounsaturated fats.

TOP with chopped nuts, chia seed jam or coconut cream instead.

A PINCH of dried chilli flakes adds a spicy hit.

BLEND in 1–2 tablespoons almond butter (or other nut butter) for an added protein boost.

FREEZE to make a healthy chocolate ice cream.

FRUIT 'BONBON' SOUP

Rather than candy confectionery, these 'bonbons' are made out of fresh fruit and are
a great way to encourage kids to find the fun in fruit and enjoy its natural sweetness.
Use as many brightly coloured fruits as you can find; I've also used a small amount
of beetroot to give a beautiful magenta colour to the soup – you can't detect the
taste at all. If you can find pink-fleshed dragon fruit by all means use that instead
of the beetroot.

SERVES 4-6

FOR THE SOUP

2 frozen bananas (you can use unfrozen ones, but frozen give an ice-creamy texture)

2 large pears, cored and cut into large chunks

1 pineapple, peeled, cored and cut into large chunks

1 thumb-sized piece of raw beetroot, peeled ✳ 200ml (7fl oz) coconut water

FOR THE 'BONBONS'

1 small papaya, cut in half and deseeded ✳ ½ small watermelon

1 dragon fruit, cut in half ✳ 2 kiwi fruit, cut in half

6–8 physalis (cape gooseberries), outer leaves removed

a few blueberries ✳ a few grapes

To make the 'bonbons', using two different sizes of melon baller, scoop out balls of papaya,
watermelon, dragon fruit and kiwi fruit. Pile the fruit balls along with the physalis, blueberries
and grapes into a bowl and chill until needed.

To make the fruit soup, place all the ingredients in a high-speed blender and blend until
a smooth, thick consistency.

To serve, pour the soup into bowls and decorate with the fruit 'bonbons' sprinkled over.

Nutrition tip

There's no better or more effective way to boost your intake of vitamin C and other antioxidants than
with this delicious fruit medley.

FREEZE the fruit soup to make a healthy ice cream.

THREAD the fruit 'bonbons' onto skewers to make mini fruit kebabs.

INSERT toothpicks into the fruit 'bonbons' and dunk them into the soup as a kind of fruit fondue.

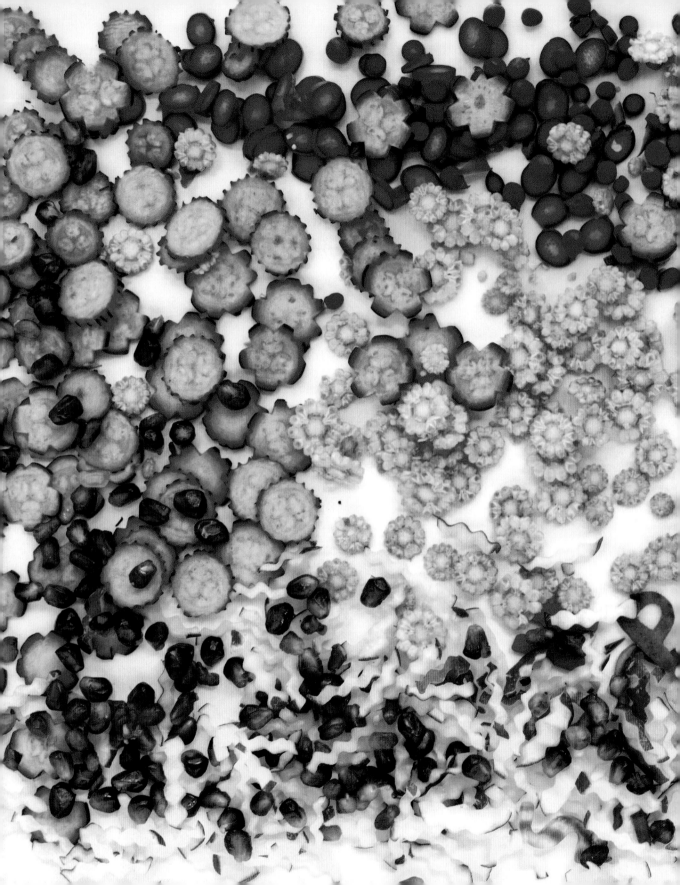

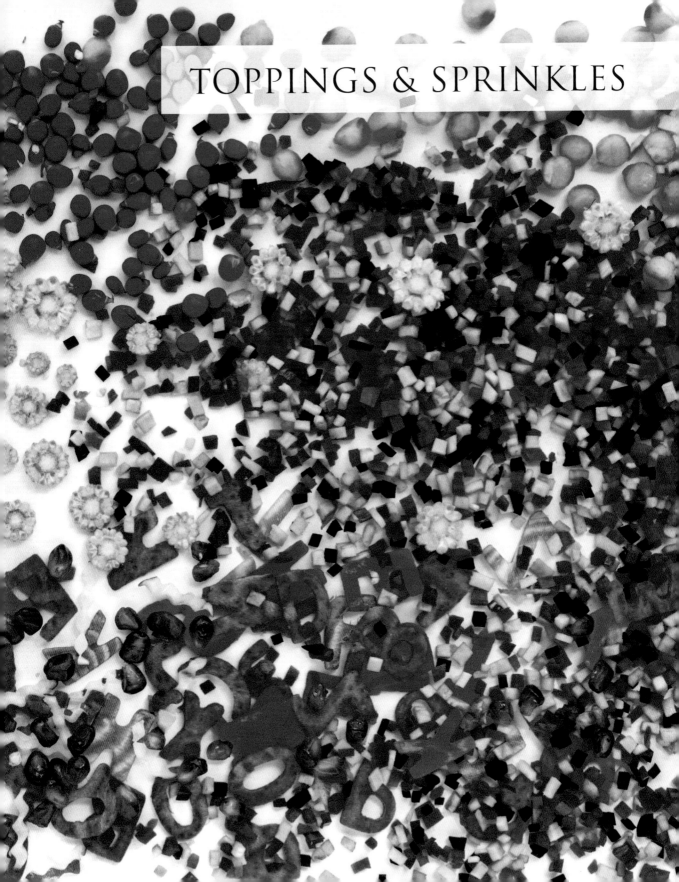

TOPPINGS & SPRINKLES

DRY SPRINKLES

1. ZA'ATAR

Sprinkle this Egyptian spice mix over soups, stews and cooked vegetables. It also makes a great flavouring for marinades and dressings. You could add other flavourings, too, including dried lemon zest and fennel pollen or, if you're planning on eating the za'atar straightaway, make it with fresh herbs instead of dried.

2 tbsp dried herbs, such as thyme, oregano and marjoram

2 tbsp toasted sesame seeds ❊ 2 tsp sumac

½ tsp sea salt

Crumble the dried herbs into a bowl, add the rest of the ingredients and mix together. If you want a finer blend, process the mixture in a coffee grinder or spice mill, or in a high-speed blender. Store in an airtight container for up to 2 months.

2. DUKKAH

This aromatic North African dry spice mix is made from toasted nuts, seeds and spices and is great mixed with olive oil as a dip, sprinkled over cooked veg, soups, stews, rice, lentils or in salad dressings, or used to flavour a yogurt marinade.

1 tsp hazelnuts ❊ 2 tsp sunflower seeds

2 tsp coriander seeds ❊ 1 tsp fennel seeds

1 tsp black onion seeds ❊ ½ tsp paprika

50g (1¾oz) Spiced Roasted Chickpeas
(omit the spices, see page 134)

salt and pepper

Gently toast the nuts and seeds (except the black onion seeds) in a large, dry frying pan until lightly golden, about 2–3 minutes. Leave to one side to cool, then season to taste with salt and pepper.

Place all the ingredients in a food processor and pulse briefly into a coarse, gritty mixture. You can continue to process it into a finer powdered nutty spice mix, if you prefer.

Store in an airtight container for up to 1 month.

3. PANCH PHORAN

Made with whole spices, this Indian spice mix is really easy to put together with equal quantities of just five ingredients. It gives a wonderful flavour and aroma to any dish requiring curry-type flavours. It's also great sprinkled over roasted veg or crushed and mixed with oil as a dip for bread, or stirred into yogurt as a marinade.

1 tbsp fenugreek seeds ❊ 1 tbsp fennel seeds

1 tbsp black onion seeds ❊ 1 tbsp nigella seeds

1 tbsp cumin seeds

Mix the seeds together and store in an airtight container for up to 2 months.

4. GARLIC SALT

Watch this become a favourite kitchen condiment and handy instant-flavour booster, minus the nasties, such as anti-caking agents, that are often found in shop-bought varieties.

10–12 garlic cloves, peeled and left whole

250g (9oz) sea salt

Preheat the oven to 65°C (150°F) Gas Mark ¼ or as low as your oven will go.

Place the garlic and salt in the bowl of a food processor and process until the garlic is chopped to a fine mince. Spread the mixture out onto a large baking tray lined with baking paper.

Place in the oven for 1 hour, or until completely crisp and dry, but don't allow the mixture to brown.

Break the salt mixture into pieces and blitz in a food processor (make sure it is clean and very well dried first) until a very fine, gritty texture.

Store in an airtight container for 2–3 months.

5. POPPED PUMPKIN SEEDS

Dried pumpkin seeds are really easy to pop. You could flavour them with extra seasonings, such as ground spices, garlic and herbs – just mix the seeds with a little oil and combine with the pumpkin seeds before toasting.

3–4 tbsp dried pumpkin seeds from a packet

salt and pepper

Heat a large, nonstick sauté pan over a medium-high heat and add the pumpkin seeds. Cover with the lid and cook for 3–4 minutes until the seeds begin to pop. If you agitate the pan while cooking, the seeds will cook more evenly and it will help them to pop. Tip the seeds onto kitchen paper and season.

Leave to cool and store in an airtight jar for up to 2 weeks.

...OR TRY ROASTED PUMPKIN SEEDS

Save your fresh pumpkin seeds to roast and sprinkle over a soup or salad, or to eat as a snack.

seeds from 1 pumpkin

1–2 tbsp olive oil or melted coconut oil

flavouring of choice, such as dried chilli flakes, ground cumin, fennel seeds, curry powder, tomato powder, onion salt, paprika, maple syrup, citrus zest, finely chopped rosemary or Parmesan

salt and pepper

Preheat the oven to 190°C (375°F) Gas Mark 5.

Clean the seeds by removing any attached flesh or membrane and rinse under cold running water. Drain well in a sieve and tip onto kitchen paper and pat dry.

Tip the seeds into a bowl and pour over the oil. Add your flavouring of choice, season to taste with salt and pepper and mix well to combine.

Spread out the seeds in a single layer on a baking tray and roast for 5–10 minutes until the seeds are lightly golden.

When roasted, tip the seeds onto kitchen paper and sprinkle with a little extra salt, if desired.

Leave to cool and use straightaway or store in an airtight jar for up to 2 weeks.

6. POPPED SAVOURY QUINOA

Popped quinoa can be flavoured to make a savoury – or sweet – sprinkle. No boiling required: simply cook the quinoa in a dry pan until popped and puffed up!

200g (7oz) quinoa

flavouring of choice, such as nutritional yeast flakes, ground turmeric, ground cumin, paprika or dried herbs

2–3 tbsp nuts or seeds, such as cashew nuts, sunflower seeds, sesame or pumpkin seeds

salt and pepper

Heat a large, nonstick sauté pan over a medium-high heat, add enough quinoa to cover the base of the pan in a thin, single layer and put on the lid. (You will need to cook the quinoa in batches.)

Lower the heat to medium and cook for 5–6 minutes, shaking the pan occasionally, until the quinoa pops and puffs up.

Tip the popped quinoa into a bowl, add your choice of flavouring and season to taste with salt and pepper. Repeat with the remaining quinoa and flavourings. Leave to cool.

Toast the nuts and seeds in the pan for 2–3 minutes, tossing the pan occasionally, until starting to colour. Leave to cool then combine with the popped flavoured quinoa.

Store in an airtight jar for up to 2 weeks.

7. GREMOLATA

Typically made with three ingredients: lemon, garlic and parsley, gremolata adds an instant brightness to any dish. Especially lovely with steamed green vegetables or on pasta.

finely grated zest of 1 lemon

1 small handful of parsley leaves

1 garlic clove, finely chopped or grated

Mix together all the ingredients until combined. Use straightaway or store in an airtight container in the fridge for up to 1 week.

8. SAVOURY GRANOLA

Not just for breakfast! This savoury version is oat-free but a handful of oats wouldn't go amiss. You could also blitz the granola in a food processor for a finer sprinkle, if preferred.

250g (9oz) mixed nuts and seeds, such as pumpkin seeds, sesame seeds, walnuts, hazelnuts, pecans and flaked almonds

2 tbsp ground flaxseeds or chia seeds

2 tsp ground spices, such a paprika, garam masala, chilli, cumin, coriander or mustard seeds

2 tbsp olive oil or melted coconut oil ✢ 3 tbsp water

salt and pepper

Preheat the oven to 180°C (350°F) Gas Mark 4.

Mix the dry ingredients in a large bowl and season to taste. Pour in the oil and measured water and stir until combined.

Spread the mixture out onto 2 baking trays in a thin, even layer. Bake for 15–20 minutes until lightly golden and crispy. You may need to stir it once or twice during baking.

Cool on a wire rack, then crumble to a coarse texture. Use straightaway or store in an airtight container for up to 2 weeks.

9. PANGRITATA

Otherwise known as 'poor man's Parmesan', and typically a mix of fried breadcrumbs, herbs and garlic. If you don't have bread to hand, dry crackers make a good substitute.

1 small handful of fresh herbs, such as rosemary, sage, marjoram and thyme, leaves only

1–2 garlic cloves, peeled and left whole

3 slices of stale bread (sourdough is ideal)

1 tbsp olive oil ✢ finely grated zest of 1 lemon

salt and pepper

Place the herbs, garlic and bread in a food processor and blitz to chunky or fine crumbs, as you prefer.

Heat the oil in a large frying pan over a medium-high heat. Add the breadcrumb mixture and fry for 3–4 minutes, turning often, until golden and crisp.

Tip onto kitchen paper, then mix in the lemon zest and season to taste. Use straightaway or store in an airtight container for up to 1 week.

DEHYDRATED SPRINKLES & POWDERS

You only need a sprinkling of dehydrated ingredients to give a great flavour boost to your cooking – use whole, crumbled or ground into powdered form. You don't need a dehydrator, a low oven works just as well.

10. HERB POWDER

Preheat the oven to 65°C (150°F) Gas Mark ¼ or as low as it will go (or follow the instructions for your dehydrator).

Arrange 2 handfuls of tender herb leaves, such as parsley, coriander or dill, in a single layer on a wire rack set inside or on a baking tray. Place in the oven for 1–1½ hours until completely dry and brittle.

Grind in batches in a spice mill, coffee grinder, food processor or high-speed blender to a fine powder. Use straightaway or store in an airtight container for 2 months. After this time the powder will start to lose its flavour and fragrance.

11. BEETROOT POWDER

Preheat the oven to 65°C (150°F) Gas Mark ¼ or as low as it will go (or follow the instructions for your dehydrator).

Very finely slice 2–3 scrubbed raw beetroots using a mandoline or sharp knife and arrange in a single layer on wire racks set inside or on baking trays. Place in the oven for 3–4 hours until completely dry and brittle.

Grind and store as for the Herb Powder.

12. CITRUS POWDER

Preheat the oven to 65°C (150°F) Gas Mark ¼ or as low as it will go (or follow the instructions for your dehydrator).

Remove the peel from 2 large oranges using a small sharp knife and taking care to leave as much of the white pith on the fruit as possible.

Place the peel in a saucepan and pour over enough cold water to cover. Bring to the boil and cook for a couple of minutes then, using a slotted spoon, lift out of the water onto kitchen paper and pat dry.

Arrange the peel in a single layer on a wire rack set inside or on a baking tray. Place in the oven for 18–24 hours until completely dry and brittle.

Grind and store as for the Herb Powder.

COOKED SPRINKLES

1. CRISPY SAGE LEAVES

These are delicate, crunchy and have a mellow, savoury taste without the heavy, camphorous flavour that puts many people off fresh sage. Great as a snack, or scattered whole or crushed over soups, pasta, salads or cooked vegetables.

4 tbsp sunflower oil ❉ 1 bunch of fresh sage, leaves only
1 tsp sea salt flakes

Heat the oil in a large frying pan until hot, add the sage leaves and fry for 2–3 seconds until crisp but without colouring. Using a slotted spoon, transfer the leaves to kitchen paper to drain then sprinkle generously with salt.

Use the sage leaves straightaway or store in an airtight container for up to 1 week.

2. OVEN-BAKED POTATO CRISPS

You can use this method to make other root vegetable crisps, including carrot, beetroot, sweet or purple potato (the latter makes a colourful addition to any dish). Try seasoning the crisps with additional flavourings – paprika, curry powder, tomato powder or Cajun spice mix are all good. Purple potatoes lose their colour slightly as you cook them but baking them on a low-ish heat will minimize colour loss.

4 potatoes, scrubbed ❉ 2 tbsp olive oil or melted coconut oil
salt and pepper

Preheat the oven to 200°C (400°F) Gas Mark 6.

Slice the potatoes very thinly using a mandoline or sharp knife. Toss in the oil and season to taste with salt and pepper.

Tip the potato slices onto large baking trays, spreading them out evenly, and bake for 30 minutes, turning once, or until cooked and crisp.

Spread out on baking or kitchen paper and leave to dry and crisp up further, about 5–10 minutes. Sprinkle with extra salt, if you like.

3. ROOT VEGETABLE ROSTI

I've included polenta to make these rosti extra-crispy. You could fry them, but I find baking is less hassle. Also try with potato, celeriac, turnip, swede or sweet potatoes.

2 tbsp olive oil or coconut oil
1 beetroot, scrubbed and coarsely grated
2 carrots, coarsely grated ❉ 1 large parsnip, coarsely grated
2 tbsp polenta ❉ salt and pepper

Preheat the oven to 220°C (425°F) Gas Mark 7. Heat the oil in 2 large baking trays.

Mix all the ingredients together in a bowl and season to taste with salt and pepper.

Form the vegetable mixture into small balls and place them on the hot baking trays. Flatten the balls with a spatula and bake for 20–30 minutes, turning once, until cooked through, lightly golden and crispy.

Drian on kitchen paper and sprinkle with extra salt, if you like, before serving.

4. CRISPY SPROUT LEAVES

Similar in flavour to kale chips, these make a tasty snack and topping. A great way to use up the outer leaves of sprouts.

350g (12oz) Brussels sprouts, trimmed and outside leaves removed, about 100g (3½oz)
2 tbsp olive oil or melted coconut oil ❉ salt and pepper

Preheat the oven to 190°C (375°F), Gas Mark 5.

Place the outer leaves from the sprouts in a bowl, toss gently in the oil and season to taste with salt and pepper.

Tip the leaves onto a large baking tray, spreading them out in an even layer, and cook for 10–15 minutes until crisp and golden around the edges.

Transfer to kitchen paper to drain. Sprinkle with a little extra salt, if you like and ideally eat straightaway.

5. SPICED ROASTED CHICKPEAS

Roasted chickpeas make a great snack and even better croûtons. These are smoky and spicy with a bit of bite.

400g (14oz) cooked dried or canned chickpeas, well drained

2 tbsp olive oil or melted coconut oil

1 tsp smoked paprika ❋ 1 tsp ground cumin

1 tsp Garlic Salt (see page 128), optional

few pinches of chilli powder ❋ salt and pepper

Preheat the oven to 200°C (400°F) Gas Mark 6.

Tip the chickpeas onto kitchen paper and rub them until completely dry, discarding any loose skins.

Place them in a bowl, pour over the oil and sprinkle with the spices and seasoning. Mix gently to coat the chickpeas.

Tip the chickpeas onto large baking trays, spread out evenly, and roast for 15–20 minutes until golden brown and crispy. Eat straightaway or store in an airtight container for up to 2 weeks.

6. MARINATED 'PANEER' BITES

Tofu absorbs flavours really well so strong flavourings and seasonings are ideal here. These crunchy, chewy nibbles taste distinctly cheesy but by all means substitute the tofu for paneer.

juice and finely grated zest of 1 lemon

1 tsp maple syrup, or sweetener of choice

½ tsp garam masala or curry powder

1 tsp Garlic Salt (see page 128) ❋ 2 tsp nutritional yeast flakes

300g (10 ½oz) tofu, drained and patted dry

1 tsp olive oil or coconut oil ❋ salt and pepper

Whisk together the lemon juice and zest, maple syrup, garam masala, garlic salt and nutritional yeast flakes then season to taste. Pour the marinade into a shallow dish or sealable plastic bag. Add the tofu and refrigerate overnight.

Drain the tofu, pat dry and cut into cubes, about 1cm/½in.

Heat the oil in a large, nonstick frying pan over a medium-high heat, add the tofu and fry until golden brown on all sides.

Tip the tofu onto kitchen paper to drain and sprinkle with a little extra salt, if necessary, before serving.

7. CAULIFLOWER STEAKS

I've used mini cauliflowers to make these 'steaks'. If you're using a large cauliflower then it's best to cook the steaks completely in the oven, or sear them first in a frying pan until lightly browned and then finish them off in a medium-hot oven. The steaks are lovely brushed with spiced or flavoured oil, such as that from a jar of sun-dried tomatoes.

2 mini cauliflowers, outer leaves removed

1–2 tbsp olive oil or coconut oil ❋ salt and pepper

Carefully slice each cauliflower into four vertical slices and keep any bits of cauli that break off to cook alongside the steaks – these bits become extra crispy and delicious! Season both sides of the steaks with salt and pepper.

Heat the oil in a large sauté pan, add the cauliflower steaks and fry until browned on both sides. Cover the pan with the lid and cook gently until tender and cooked through. Transfer the steaks to kitchen paper to drain and serve warm.

8. SPICED PARSNIP CRISPS

These oven-baked crisps are easy to make and can be adapted to any root vegetable, such as carrot, beetroot or sweet potato. Season with additional flavourings, such as curry powder, tomato powder or Cajun spice mix, if you like.

2–3 large parsnips, scrubbed

2 tbsp olive oil or melted coconut oil

½ tsp smoked sweet paprika ❋ ½ tsp ground cumin

salt and pepper

Preheat the oven to 200°C (400°F) Gas Mark 6.

Slice the parsnips very thinly using a mandoline or sharp knife. Toss with the oil, paprika and cumin and season to taste with salt and pepper.

Tip the parsnips onto large baking trays, spreading them out evenly, and bake for 30 minutes, turning once, or until cooked through and crisp.

Spread out on baking or kitchen paper and leave to dry and crisp up further, about 5-10 minutes. Sprinkle with extra salt, if you like.

DRIZZLES

1. GREEN HERB OIL

A fragrant oil that can be made with any combination of herbs: the more you use, the thicker the oil will be, almost becoming a paste. Alternatively, for a clear, bright green oil, steep it in the fridge for 2–3 days and then strain and discard the herbs. Great for drizzling over soups, pasta, toasted bread, cooked vegetables or salads. I've added a small green chilli and garlic to give the oil a bit of extra oomph.

2 large of handfuls of mixed green herbs, such as coriander, basil, parsley and rosemary

1 garlic clove, peeled and left whole

1 small green chilli, deseeded ❖ 150ml (5fl oz) olive oil

Place the herbs (use the tender stems as well but avoid tough rosemary stalks), garlic and chilli in the bowl of a food processor and pulse briefly until roughly chopped.

With the motor running, slowly trickle in the oil and process to a thick, smooth, almost paste-like consistency. Pour in extra oil, if you prefer a thinner consistency. Store in a sterilized airtight jar in the fridge for up to 1 week.

2. FRESH HERB PESTO

Traditionally made in a pestle and mortar, by pounding garlic with salt, fresh herbs and pine nuts and finally stirring in oil and Parmesan but the method below is much quicker. This is a cheese-free version, but do add a handful of finely grated Parmesan or vegan hard cheese, if you wish.

1 large handful of tender-leaf herbs, such as basil, parsley, mint, dill, tarragon and/or coriander

100ml (3½fl oz) extra virgin olive oil

50–70g (1¾–2½oz) nuts or seeds, such as pine nuts, almonds, walnuts, pistachio nuts or sunflower seeds

2 garlic cloves, peeled and left whole ❖ salt and pepper

Put all the ingredients into the bowl of a food processor and blitz or pulse to a grainy sauce-like consistency.

Season with salt and pepper and add more oil if too thick. Store in a sterilized airtight jar in the fridge for up to 1 week.

3. SRIRACHA SAUCE

This Asian-style, spicy-sweet, hot chilli sauce is addictive – before you know it you are squeezing it over everything! It often contains sugar, monosodium glutamate (MSG) and a handful of other E numbers; this version avoids the additives.

250g (9oz) red or green jalapeño chillies

250g (9oz) small red sweet peppers ❖ 6–7 garlic cloves, peeled

100ml (3½fl oz) apple cider vinegar ❖ 3 tbsp tomato purée

3–4 tbsp maple syrup, or sweetener of choice

2 tbsp soy sauce or *nama shoyu* ❖ salt and pepper

Place all the ingredients in a high-speed blender and process to a smooth, thin paste.

Tip the paste into a small saucepan. Heat to simmering point. Cook gently for 10–15 minutes until reduced and thickened. Season and tweak the salty, sweet flavours to your taste.

Leave to cool completely and store in a sterilized airtight jar in the fridge for up to 3 weeks.

4. GAZPACHO SALSA

This fresh-tasting salsa is great with the addition of finely chopped chilli for a bit of heat, or a few chopped black olives.

¼ cucumber, finely chopped

100g (3½oz) ripe tomatoes, finely chopped

½ red pepper, deseeded and finely chopped

1 celery stick, finely chopped

1 small garlic clove, finely chopped

1 spring onion, finely chopped

1 small handful of parsley or basil, leaves finely chopped

salt and pepper

Gently mix together all the ingredients in a bowl. Season to taste with salt and pepper, cover, and refrigerate until required. It will keep for 2–3 days in the fridge. Mix the salsa again just before serving.

5. RAW ALMOND YOGURT

This plain, creamy yogurt is also lovely with the seeds scraped from half a vanilla pod or a splash of vanilla extract. To use this recipe in savoury dishes, simply leave out the sweetener.

175g (6oz) raw (skin on) almonds

450ml (16fl oz) coconut water

1 tbsp coconut syrup or maple syrup, or sweetener of choice

½ tsp vegan probiotic powder

pinch of sea salt

Soak the almonds in water for 24 hours until softened, then drain and peel away the skins.

Place the soaked almonds with the other ingredients in a high-speed blender and blend on high until smooth and creamy – this may take a while if your blender isn't very powerful.

Pour the almond milk into a bowl or jar (strain first if not completely smooth). Cover with kitchen paper or a cloth. Leave at room temperature for 6–12 hours until thickened to a yogurt-like consistency.

Use straightaway or keep in the fridge in an airtight container for 5–7 days.

6. GREEN CASHEW DRIZZLE

Swirl this green drizzle on to soup, a vegetable dish, or use it to dress a salad. Blend in ½ small garlic clove for a garlic mayo-type sauce, or ½ green chilli for a spicy kick.

100g (3½oz) cashew nuts

1 small handful of mixed greens and herbs, such as parsley, mint, pea shoots, spinach and basil, leaves roughly chopped

1 spring onion, roughly chopped

juice and finely grated zest of 1 lemon

salt and pepper (to taste)

Soak the cashews in water for at least 1 hour until softened, then drain.

Place the soaked nuts in a high-speed blender with the other ingredients and pour over just enough water to cover. Blend on high until smooth and the consistency of single cream – this may take a while if your blender isn't powerful. Season to taste.

Use straightaway or keep in the fridge in an airtight container for 2–3 days.

7. MACADAMIA CREAM CHEESE

Soaked macadamia nuts blend easily to form a surprisingly good mild-tasting vegan 'cheese', which is similar in texture to a crumbly goats' cheese and can be flavoured with herbs, garlic or spices such as paprika and Za'atar (see page 128). This makes a round cheese but you could form it into a log shape or small balls and then roll them in the flavouring, crushed nuts or seeds.

250g (9oz) shelled macadamia nuts

250–300ml (9–10fl oz) water

2 tbsp melted coconut oil

1 tsp vegan probiotic powder

pinch of sea salt

Soak the macadamia nuts in water for 3–4 hours until softened, then drain.

Place the soaked nuts in a high-speed blender with the measured water and coconut oil and blend on high until thick, smooth and creamy – this may take a while if your blender isn't very powerful.

Pour the macadamia milk into a bowl or jar (strain it first if not completely smooth) and cover with kitchen paper or a cloth. Leave at room temperature for 6–12 hours (depending on how warm the environment is) until thickened to a yogurt-like consistency.

Strain the mixture through a nut milk bag or muslin-lined sieve set over a bowl. Leave to drain, pressing it down occasionally to extract as much liquid as possible, until the texture of a crumbly goats' cheese.

Remove the nut cheese from the bag or muslin and use straightaway or keep in the fridge in an airtight container for up to 1 week.

OTHER STOCKS, SAUCES & LIQUIDS

PASSATA (NOT SHOWN)

Need to use up a glut of tomatoes? This is an ideal base for a quick soup or stew. Thinned down passata makes an almost instant gazpacho as well as the perfect Bloody Mary base.

1 tbsp olive oil

800g (1lb 12oz) ripe tomatoes, roughly chopped

4–5 garlic cloves, finely chopped ❊ ½ tsp sugar

salt and pepper

Heat the oil in a large saucepan and add the tomatoes and garlic. Cover with the lid and cook gently for 10–15 minutes until the tomatoes have softened and rendered their liquid.

Add the sugar, season well and simmer, uncovered, for a further 10–15 minutes until reduced and thickened.

Leave to cool slightly, then press the sauce through a fine sieve – you should be left with a smooth, thick pulp. You could also blend the sauce at this point but the passata will be thicker.

Store in an airtight container in the fridge for up to 1 week, or freeze for up to 1 month.

1. VEGAN DASHI

Traditionally, the Japanese stock dashi uses kombu (seaweed) and bonito (tuna) flakes. This vegan version uses dried shiitake mushrooms and kelp powder to give a similar umami flavour.

1 litre (1¾ pints) water ❊ 70g (2½oz) dried shiitake mushrooms

1–2 tsp kelp or kombu powder

Pour the water into a large saucepan. Heat until warm.

Put the mushrooms in a large bowl and pour over the warm (not hot) water. Soak for 3–4 hours then strain the mushrooms (keep them to use in a soup) and reserve the mushroom stock.

Whisk the kelp or kombu powder into the mushroom stock until dissolved. Strain through a very fine or muslin-lined sieve to remove any grit.

Store in an airtight container in the fridge for up to 1 week.

2. RAW CASHEW CREAM – THREE WAYS

Most types of nut can be transformed into a raw vegan cream, but if you're not using cashews you'll need to soak them for longer – up to 24 hours – to achieve a similar smooth and creamy consistency.

This makes a thick double cream-like consistency. If you require a thinner cream, just add more liquid such as water, coconut water or lemon juice.

100g (3½oz) cashew nuts ❊ 100ml (3½fl oz) water

pinch of sea salt

Soak the cashews in water for at least 1 hour until softened, then drain.

Place the soaked nuts in a high-speed blender with the water and salt and blend on high until smooth and the consistency of double cream – this may take a while if your blender isn't very powerful.

Use straightaway or keep in the fridge in an airtight container for 2–3 days.

Variations:

VANILLA CASHEW CREAM

To make a sweetened vanilla version, use coconut water instead of plain water and add 1 teaspoon maple syrup, or sweetener of choice, the seeds of ½ vanilla pod or ½ teaspoon vanilla extract to the blender with the soaked cashews. Continue with the recipe as described, above.

SOURED CASHEW CREAM

To make a vegan soured cream, add 1 tablespoon lemon juice, 1 teaspoon finely grated lemon zest and 1 teaspoon raw apple cider vinegar to the blender with the soaked cashews. Continue with the recipe as described, above.

3. ORANGE BLOSSOM OR ROSE WATER

It's easier to get hold of beautifully fragrant rose petals to make a floral water than it is to obtain fresh orange blossoms, but whichever one you use make sure that the flowers haven't been sprayed with chemicals.

This recipe makes a delicately flavoured and fragrant infused water, which is not as strong as shop-bought versions so you may need to increase the amount you use. Distilled water can be bought in most chemist shops.

2 handfuls of untreated orange blossoms or rose petals
about 200ml (7fl oz) distilled water

Pick the flowers early in the day and wash thoroughly in cool water to remove any dirt. Separate the petals and dry thoroughly then crush using a pestle and mortar.

Place the crushed petals in a large jar and pour the water over to cover. Put a lid on the jar and place in a sunny position for 5–7 days or until the water becomes infused with the flavour and fragrance of the petals. When ready, strain and bottle into sterilized jars and store in a cool, dark place for 1–2 weeks.

4. COCONUT MILK

You can use either fresh or dried coconut, but fresh will give a better flavour. The flesh of a young coconut is softer and blends more easily, but all options yield a plausible and healthier alternative to canned coconut milk.

1 fresh coconut, halved, reserving the water, or 200g (7oz)
unsweetened dried shredded or desiccated coconut
300–450ml (10–16fl oz) cold water

If using fresh coconut, cut away the flesh from the shell and put it into a high-speed blender with the coconut water and the smaller amount of measured water. Blend to a pulp, adding extra water if the milk is too thick, or if your blender struggles.

If using dried coconut, use hot water rather than cold as it helps to soften and rehydrate it. Put the dried coconut into a high-speed blender with the larger amount of measured water. Blend to a pulp, adding extra water if the milk is too thick, or if your blender struggles to process the mixture.

Pour the coconut milk into a nut milk bag or a muslin-lined sieve set over a bowl. Drain, squeezing the pulp to extract all the liquid. Discard the dry pulp or use as body scrub.

Store in an airtight container in the fridge for up to 1 week.

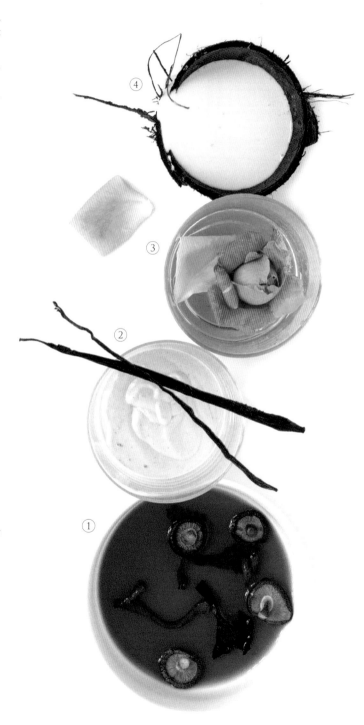

INDEX

An Hachette UK Company
www.hachette.co.uk

First published in Great Britain in 2017 by Mitchell Beazley,
a division of Octopus Publishing Group Ltd
Carmelite House
50 Victoria Embankment
London EC4Y 0DZ
www.octopusbooks.co.uk

ISBN 978-1-78472-209-8

A CIP catalogue record for this book is available from the
British Library.

Printed and bound in China

10 9 8 7 6 5 4 3 2 1

Publishing Director Stephanie Jackson
Art Director Yasia Williams-Leedham
Editor Pollyanna Poulter
Copy Editor Nicola Graimes
Nutritionist Angela Dowden
Assistant Production Manager Marina Maher
Photographer Amber Locke

AMBER WOULD LIKE TO THANK…

Firstly, I'd like to thank Stephanie Jackson, publishing director
at Octopus books, for giving me the opportunity to write and
photograph my second book and extend my printed 'voice'
into the repertoire of soups. As a 'veg evangelist' it's wonderful
to have another literary vehicle to share my passion for fruit
and veg and illustrate how delicious and easy it is to 'get more
of the good stuff down'!

Secondly, I'd like to thank the amazing support team at
Octopus who have assembled and crafted this book into
what you see today. In particular, art director Yasia Williams
for working her creative magic on the beautiful design and
layout of this book and for her artistic guidance with styling
and photography, and to my editor Polly Poulter for her
endless patience and gracious editing of me and my rambling
manuscript! Thanks also to PR supremos Karen Baker and
Siobhan McDermott, to copy editor Nicola Graimes and to all
the other troupers who worked so hard on this book as part
of the 'Savour' team.

Words cannot express the gratitude I feel to my parents for
raising me to understand the importance of good food, home
cooking and an appreciation of the beauty of Nature. Thank
you to my mother for helping me source crockery and allowing
me to constantly plunder her cupboards for cutlery and
props, and thank you to my father for a never-ending supply
of freshly-painted backgrounds, textured surfaces and my
random requests for spray painted leaves, fruit and vegetables!

To my partner Mark for his constant support, encouragement
and faith in me and for always pushing me to step outside my
comfort zones!

Finally, huge, massive and time-less thanks to all the people
that support my work and to all my followers on social media,
without whom non of this would have been possible.

Love and veggie blessings to you all x